Visualization - p33

Release Your Superhero

Optimism
p5
opt. visualystn
Affirmation - p8

Resilience
p15 - powerfully (Method)

Content of a talk p60

lasting impressions from talks : p61

Talking to "VIP's"

Release Your Superhero

How to Shed the Villains and Soar in Business and in Life

A Coach's Recipe for Reaching Your True Potential

Ed DeCosta

ACKNOWLEDGEMENT

In my first book, Ascend, A Coach's Roadmap for Taking Your Performance to New Heights, I gave sincere thanks to many of the people who have inspired me, challenged me and loved me in my life. I failed to mention a man to whom I owe an immeasurable debt of gratitude: Dr. Thomas P. Lombardi.

Tom is my father-in-law. I met him in 1981 as I was trying to get his daughter Linda to become my girlfriend (and later to become and remain my wife). Needless to say, Linda was a "hard-sell". It took years of pursuit and every ounce of creativity, charm and charisma that I could produce to earn the honor to spend my life with Linda. That being said, it took quite a while longer to win over my future father-in-law. Only

now, 34 years later and the father of an 18-year-old daughter, can I fully appreciate where Tom was coming from as he made me jump through numerous hoops to win his trust.

He is now a great friend and trusted confidant, as well as the loving grandfather of our three children. We tease each other constantly, as only two men with deep respect for one another are able to.

Firstly, I am grateful to Tom, and of course my mother-in-law Estelle, for the gift of my family. Without them, there would be no Linda. Without Linda, there would be no David, Brian or Laura.

Beyond that, Tom has taught me how to lead a family, how to work hard and pray earnestly, how to laugh when it is time to laugh and cry when it is time to cry. Following Tom's example, I have been able to face and overcome many challenges, both personal and professional.

Using Tom as a model, I have become a better father, a better teacher and a better husband. In the interest of transparency, I must also acknowledge that he would be the first to point out that I have a long way to go! He's right about that too.

I am proud to be part of his legacy.

TABLE OF CONTENTS

FOREWORD: TRUE SUPERHEROES ARE MADE, NOT BORN

I have a confession to make. To be more precise, a *few* confessions.

For one, I wasn't born on Krypton.

For another, I was not bitten by a radioactive spider. I also have to admit I have never been bombarded by gamma rays or cosmic rays. And no, I'm not even a super-brilliant billionaire inventor who built a flying metal suit in order to battle evildoers (although the engineer in me certainly wants a good look at that suit!).

All of the above scenarios, as I'm sure many of you reading this are aware, are the "origin stories" behind some of the most popular superheroes drawing in crowds today. I'm talking Superman, Spiderman, the Hulk, the Fantastic Four and Iron Man.

Me, I'm just Flesh and Bone Ed. And that's perfectly fine. Because, frankly, I'm a fan of the self-made superhero.

The best example of the self-made superhero? Batman. He's just a guy, right? Granted, he's a guy with a lot of money...but you know what I mean. Sure he's got a Batmobile, a Batcave, a Batsuit, maybe even Bat-underwear, who knows? What he *doesn't* have, however, is superhuman powers. He can't fly, he can't break down walls, he can't turn invisible or grow thirty feet tall. Nope, he only has his God-given brains and brawn to take care of business. But you know what? That's enough to get the job done for him.

More importantly, it's enough to do the job for *all* of us.

And by all of us, I mean *all* of us. If you're reading this book, that, to me, puts us in the same tribe - that tribe of people that are interested in personal development and ongoing improvement in our professions as well as our personal relationships. Simply put, you're the kind of person who never loses an appetite for making more of yourself. You want to be…well, a superhero.

Surprisingly, not everybody does. Many people are very happy to settle for the status quo. They get to a place where maybe they're making a certain amount of money in a job they know inside out and they're content to remain in that place. Or maybe they've gotten married and figure that's the end of the story when it comes to relationship-building. Whatever the details might be, these are people looking for a comfortable resting place, rather than a challenging life journey that will dare them to grow and change in positive ways.

Now, these aren't bad people. A lot of them are simply afraid – afraid that they are somehow lacking in what it takes to make that kind of journey. They get intimidated, because there's a great myth about people who are very successful – that they are somehow gifted with superior talents that grant them an easy path to prosperity in all things. The implication is, as the word "gifted" implies, they didn't really *earn* these talents – they were just lucky enough to be born with them.

Well, here's a little secret I'd like to share: The more "gifted" people I meet, the more I'm convinced there's far fewer *actually* gifted people than we would like to believe.

In other words, there are a heck of a lot more Batmen than Supermen!

The successful weren't born with powers and abilities far above those of ordinary mortals – no, they were born crying for their mommies, just like you and me.

The difference comes in what they *do* with themselves. They work really hard. They never lose the burning passion to continually improve themselves and their circumstances. And they always follow through on what's important to their goals. It's not that they're unhappy or chronic malcontents – *they just want to keep getting better.*

It is precisely this attitude that turns them into superheroes.

I strongly believe that all of us have a superhero somewhere inside of us – a superior being who can fly high, accomplish great deeds and inspire others along the way. I also believe that when you bring that superhero to life, you too can pack the punch of the Hulk, fly high like Iron Man and or maneuver around the most dangerous obstacles with an incredible series of flips and rolls like the Black Widow.

But there's a catch. You can't make all that happen by sitting on your backside.

No, if you really want to reach the peak of your personal power and become everything you can possibly be, again, that takes work. That work may seem hard at the start, but once you turn it into a daily habit and once you begin to see the many rewards it delivers to your personal and professional life...well, that's when the work becomes a genuine pleasure.

In the following pages, you're going to learn about the areas of life I believe you need to address in order to "Release Your Superhero." Some of the things I talk about you may already be doing. Some may be things you've thought about doing but just never had the motivation to tackle. And some may be things that will jolt you into surprising realizations about just what's been blocking your path to life success.

So – are you ready to try your superhero cape on for size? I'm betting you are, or you wouldn't be reading this book.

To me, it comes down to this – we are all faced with a choice. We can stay safely nestled in our "secret identities" and remain blissfully unaware of the super suits we have tucked away underneath our street clothes - or we can, instead, become what I like to call "the best version of ourselves" and create a wave of super change both in ourselves and the world at large.

When you release your superhero, you release an awesome force into the world that will help you reach your goals faster than a speeding bullet...make your business more powerful than a locomotive...and allow you to leap over life's hurdles with a single bound!

Do I exaggerate? Maybe a little. But just wait – after you've released your inner superhero, you won't be able to stop yourself from shouting...

"HOLY TRANSFORMATION, BATMAN!"

PART 1
YOUR ORIGIN STORY:
POWER PRINCIPLES TO BUILD ON

> *"Success has always been easy to measure. It is the distance between one's origins and one's final achievement."*
> — MICHAEL KORDA

As I said, every superhero has his or her own "origin story." That origin story is important, because if the beginning isn't good, it's awfully hard to correct your course down the line – so I want to make sure yours is the right one. Before you even think about putting on a mask, a cape and tights, you have to begin developing the right mindset that will render you invulnerable to setbacks, frustrations and overwhelming obstacles.

That's why, in this section of the book, I'm going to focus on some elemental "power principles" I believe you need to take on board at the very start of your transformation into "Super You" – because they will help you create a winning mindset that will help you triumph over evil… or at least, keep it on the outside looking in!

ON BECOMING

On November 28th, 2012, I received some very bad news: Zig Ziglar had passed away at the age of 86.

For 30 years, I had been an avid fan of this legendary figure in the self-help industry. I read his books, listened to his tapes and, in general, soaked up all the wisdom he had to share.

The primary lesson this great man had to offer? In a word, *optimism*. And boy, did he believe in the concept. He's the guy who said, "I'd take my last two dollars and buy a money belt" and "I'd even go after Moby Dick in a rowboat, and take the tartar sauce with me!"

Yes, ladies and gentlemen, that's an optimist - something I strive to be in every waking moment. I even describe myself as "Optimist-In-Charge" on my Facebook page.

There are a lot of misconceptions about practicing the art of positive thinking. Some people think it means you're delusional, walking around thinking everything is going to go your way, even if, when you're crossing the street, a runaway truck is inches away from turning you into a human pancake.

Well, okay, if that were to happen to me, I might think to myself, "Well, maybe the truck will run out of gas in the next two seconds," but, in general, positive thinking isn't about believing everything is wonderful. It's about believing you have the ability to make everything *better.* When you approach a situation with your energy concentrated on positive thoughts, you find yourself focusing on the methods and attitudes that will bring improvement. And even if that improvement doesn't happen, you don't walk away feeling defeated. Instead, you immediately start focusing on how you can bring about positive change in the next situation. This is an incredible asset to take with you through life, because, no matter what you do, setbacks and problems will plague you at one time or another. So the question becomes, how do we deal with those unpleasant occurrences in the most productive way?

The answer? Positive thinking.

Without it, you lose your best chance at creating the outcomes you're after. Negative thinking certainly does nothing for you. When you walk into a situation already feeling defeated, guess what? Nine times out of ten, you'll end up defeating yourself. You'll lack confidence and you won't be focused on the things you need to do to get you what you want. Instead, you'll actually end up behaving in ways that will completely sabotage your success.

This is best illustrated by one of the most famous routines that the late comedian Danny Thomas used to perform back in the glory days of nightclubs. I don't have his delivery, but here's my version:

A guy driving late at night gets a flat tire in the middle of nowhere. He opens the trunk to pull out the spare and finds out it's also flat. He doesn't have a cell phone, because, when Danny Thomas told this story, it hadn't been invented yet.

So the guy, already in a horrible mood, has to find help. He sees a farmhouse in the distance and begins walking towards it, figuring he can use the phone there. As he's walking, however, he starts thinking, "It's late, I'm going to wake these people up. But I just have to use their phone, it won't be that big a deal."

He keeps walking. His anxiety increases. "What if they're angry that I woke them up? Maybe they just got to sleep and I'm completely wrecking their night. That won't be good."

6

He walks a little further and continues this line of thought. "They probably won't even let me use the phone, they'll be so mad. I bet these people won't help me at all and I'll have to walk all the way back to the car with nothing to show for it. I'll be stuck out on the road all night."

Now he's getting furious. "Who do these people think they are? I'm only knocking on their door in the middle of the night because I'm desperate for help! I mean, it's not my fault the tire went flat! These are some kind of jerks that wouldn't help out a guy stranded out in the middle of nowhere – just because they lost five minutes of sleep!"

In a rage, he finally reaches the door of the farmhouse and pounds on it with all his might. The lights quickly come on and a sleepy-looking man in his bathrobe opens the door. "Yes?" he asks.

The guy yells "WHO NEEDS YOUR STUPID HELP ANYWAY?" and storms away.

So that's the power of negative thinking for you. Obviously, if our stranded driver had been more hopeful about the possibility of help, he would have had a chance of getting it. But by completely discounting that possibility, by painting a totally ridiculous negative picture instead, he assured himself...of the worst possible result!

That's why being a positive thinker is so critical to your daily routine – and why I'd like to share my three steps to becoming one.

Step 1: Visualize Success

Many times, people who are pessimists won't tell you they're pessimists – they'll describe themselves as "realists." And in their view, success isn't realistic – or at the very least, not worth considering. That means before they encounter difficult or challenging circumstances, they go in without a positive intention, believing that's just wishful thinking. It's not – it's focusing on creating a great outcome. When you allow yourself to have a positive intention, you can also see what steps need to be taken to realize your goals. Always visualize what you want to happen – to jumpstart the process of thinking about how to make it happen.

Step 2: Reinforce Your Visualization

Act on your positive intentions by doing daily affirmations. These are positive statements that you read to yourself or even out loud each and every day. Doing this will literally program your mind to think in a positive way. Lest you think this is what cults do to turn members into robots, remember this is not anyone else programming your mind – this is *you* making positive statements about how you're going to conduct yourself and what outcomes you expect to get as a result.

Affirmations may seem silly to you – but have you ever heard the expression, "Force of Habit?" It's a very powerful force – but to make positive thinking a habit, you have to consciously reinforce it over and over again. Affirmations do that. They help you flip that switch in your head so that you begin to react to disappointment in a very different way. Instead of becoming depressed or even despondent, you instead continue looking for positive solutions. Optimists don't quit. Optimists don't give up. Optimists say, "This failure is a temporary state, and I will learn from it. I will grow and become strong, so, in fact, this is good news for me."

Step 3: Analyze Yourself

Every garden needs weeding if it's going to thrive – and your mind needs its own form of "weeding" as well, if you're truly going to be a successful optimist.

If you reflexively have a discouraging thought in a certain circumstance – one that's really not at all justified by the facts – identify it and set a trap for it. That trap is merely examining how that discouraging thought affects your actions. For example, when you go to ask for more money from a client or a boss, your initial impulse might be to think to yourself, "I'm probably not going to get it." That thought, in turn, might make you less aggressive in arguing your case for the extra money and give up at the first turndown without a fight.

Fight that ingrained response by preparing a counter-argument to the recurring discouraging thought. Let's go back to the example of asking for more money. Let's say you caught yourself thinking that you're not going to get the extra money before you even asked for it. Then you could say to yourself in response, "Maybe if I think of ways to explain why the extra money is justified, I'll have a better shot. And maybe, if I don't get the extra money from them, I should look around for a different situation where I'll get paid what I deserve." That sets your mind working on positive ways to resolve the situation, rather than simply gearing up for disappointment.

It's not enough to deny negative thoughts – that's just repression, which rarely works. Instead, analyze your bad feelings and how they impact your behavior. Argue with them, instead of letting them rule your attitude. And finally, help yourself understand why negative thoughts aren't helpful to your efforts – if anything, they're counter-productive. I even advocate that you write down on index cards positive counterpoints to recurring negative thoughts; that way, you're armed in advance when they strike.

Here's another great technique I'll share with you. When positive thinking fails you and you can't imagine yourself overcoming an obstacle or difficult situation, instead imagine what someone you really admire would do if that person were you. For me, I might do that with Zig Ziglar. I could wonder, "How would he deal with these circumstances? How would he feel? How would he try to turn things around?" And then I would do it, whatever it was I imagined.

Whoever your role models are, use them and picture how they would handle the situation, like you were watching a scene in a movie. Visualize success through them if you can't find the answers in yourself at the moment. Often, that's all the inspiration you need to persevere.

At the end of each of these chapters, I'm going to provide a special summary so you can understand how each of these topics contributes to releasing your inner superhero. As you complete each chapter and put its tenets to work, you can keep track of each "superpower" you acquire as a result.

With that in mind, here's your first "Super Scorecard":

SUPER SCORECARD #1

Superpower:	**Optimism**
Allows you to:	**See and Create Great Results**
Obtained by:	**Visualizations, Affirmations and Self-Examination**
Arch Enemy:	**Pessimism**

Final note: Did you know the word "pessimism" didn't even exist for about a hundred years after "optimism" entered the English language? It's true – "optimism" became a word in the 17th century, while "pessimism" didn't show up until the 18th. So let's consider pessimism a modern invention – one that we can easily dispose of!

THE POWER OF PURPOSE

Can I ask you a question?

I hope so, because I'm a big believer in asking them. As an executive coach, asking questions is essential to determining where my clients currently are along their professional paths and what they need to do to up their game and reach the next level of achievement. These questions usually take the form of "What," "How" and "Why" questions.

The simplest ones for people to deal with are usually the "What" questions. "What" questions usually call for straightforward answers that are easy to respond to; some of the ones I ask are, "What are your plans?" "What are your dreams?" and "What do you want to accomplish?" These are the kinds of questions we usually ask ourselves on a daily basis, so the answers are readily available.

"How" questions, such as "How are you going to achieve your ambitions?" can obviously be a little trickier - because the clients may not have figured out just how they're going to make certain things happen. Still, they've obviously given it some thought and are comfortable talking through various ways of getting things done.

The third kind of question – the "Why" questions – can really land hard, however, and give my clients pause. Think about it – do you understand why you're on your specific life track? Do you know what's behind your ambitions and passions? You may not – a lot of people don't. That's because it's not as necessary to consider the "Why" of things as it is the "What" and "How." Often, unless somebody asks, you don't bother to worry about the reasons things are the way they are in your life.

But you should.

That's the question I want to ask you, the one I mentioned at the beginning of this chapter: *"What is your 'Why?'"*

To be more specific, why are you where you are? Why do you have the ambitions you do? Why are you happy – or unhappy? Why have you chosen the relationships you have, why do you live where you live, why are you doing what you do for a living?

Understanding your "Why" is vital to uncovering your real motivation – it helps you understand and connect with your fundamental principles, values, your truest sense of identity, where you derive your self-worth and key into what makes you unique. But to fully tap into your "Why," you have to approach it like a little child, asking "Why?" over and over again until you feel you have the right answer, the answer that makes the most sense to you.

Your "Why" is about who you are at your deepest level.

And that's why, when you get in touch with your "Why," you can easily end up changing your life course completely – because, for the first time, you've pushed yourself to see clearly who you are and what you want out of life. Of course, it's just as likely that the opposite can happen – your "Why" may lead you to recommit to your present path with a new burst of motivation and energy – because you discovered the essential part of you that has guided you towards where you are, which spurs you on to continue on your desired journey.

So yes, "Why" is the most crucial question to answer – and the hardest. But if you're willing to go through the process, you'll discover what you need to do – and how to get it done. And you'll endure that process gladly. As the great philosopher Fredrich Nietzsche once said, "He who has a why to live for can bear almost any how."

Most importantly, your "Why" will lead you to your purpose – and that's where you'll find your real power. Everyone wants to know what their calling is, what they're meant to do here on earth, what the person they are supposed to be looks like. But too many people never get in touch with their authentic selves. Too many simply grab onto what's in reach and live life from the outside in, rather than the inside out. They chase money. They chase fleeting pleasures. They even embrace needless pain, thinking it makes them better people. And they end up living false and unsatisfying lives, lives that defy their purposes instead of serve them.

I teach at the local university and the students there are naturally nervous about what they're going to end up doing to do for a living after they graduate. Purpose is very much on their minds – as is survival! Now, they know I'm an executive coach, not a career coach - but they still ask me for career advice from time to time.

My answer? Well, as you may have guessed from the rest of this chapter, I ask them questions. To be more specific, I've developed a three question sequence which I believe can help anybody zero in on their purpose, at least from a professional standpoint.

Question 1: What do you *enjoy* doing?

This first question is the most important one. I firmly subscribe to the old saying, "Do what you love, love what you do, and you'll never work a day in your life." So think about what you like to do so much that you end up losing yourself in it, to the point where hours can go by without you noticing. Think about what you would gladly do for free if money was no object. So - what puts *you* "in the zone" and makes you feel fulfilled? If you have a strong answer to this question, you're off to a great start.

Question 2: Are you any good at it - and do you have any talents or gifts in this particular area?

Let's say your answer to the first question was that you love to play the violin, you could play the instrument for hours and never get bored. But let's also say that maybe every time you do play the violin - the neighbors think stray cats are having a screaming contest out in a nearby alley!

In other words, it's great if you love to play the violin – but not so great if you can't tell a sour note from a good one. That's why you need to match your skills and gifts with something you love to do.

What gifts? I'm talking about your natural skills, things you do well intuitively, without much effort, and that you're noticed for. Do you get complimented on your writing? Your computer skills? Your speaking abilities? Your athletic ability? Is there an aspect of those talents that matches up with something you love to do? For instance, maybe you love basketball, but you're only 4'8" – is there a behind-the-scenes role you could play in the sport? Or another sport more forgiving of your height that you also enjoy?

Keep in mind, you may not have mastery of a specific profession or activity – but you may at the same time possess the natural skills that will make it easy for you to gain that mastery. For example, becoming a lawyer may seem a daunting task, but if you're good at reading, writing, logic, and debating, you should do well in law school. However, if you hate reading or arguing over arcane minutiae, your experience won't be a whole lot of fun.

Question 3: Can I make a living doing it?

The world has its economic realities; you've got to get paid for what you love to do, unless you relegate it to a hobby outside of work hours. Otherwise, you have an obligation to support yourself, your family if you have one, as well as contributing to the common good with your work.

Still, as I said, the first question is the most important one. Do something you love to do. Don't settle. Follow your intuition. Follow your passion. Follow your heart. Even if you think your dream is outlandish, you owe to yourself to try. As an old song puts it, "There's nothing to be ashamed of if you stub your toe on the moon."

Did you know comedy legend Bob Newhart, trying to be practical, studied to be an accountant for his initial career choice? It didn't go so well - in his own words, "The reason I was never a Certified Public

Accountant was because it would require passing a test - which I would not have been able to do." Becoming a comic made him a multi-millionaire instead.

You never know. And the only way you can know is to *do*. So don't give up until you've found something that can answer all three of my questions. And, by the way, it's never too late to find the right answer. Your adult life can have a happy, prosperous and productive second act, even if the first one was the wrong answer to your "Why."

All it takes is tapping into the Power of Purpose.

As one of my favorite authors, Mark Twain, once said, "The two most important days in your life are the day you are born and the day you find out why." If that second day hasn't happened yet – start working towards it now!

SUPER SCORECARD #2

Superpower:	**Purposefulness**
Allows you to:	**Stay Motivated and Focused, Be Fulfilled**
Obtained by:	**Self-Examination and Exploration**
Arch Enemy:	**Aimlessness**

I LOVE WIGS

Before you ask, I don't love wigs because I suddenly went as bald as Dr. Phil and need some head cover.

That's because I'm not talking about *those* kinds of wigs, the kind that somebody like Beyonce wears. I don't think my wife Linda would like it if she caught me wearing one of those. No, I'm talking about *WIGs*. And they're generally hairless.

Before you get even more confused, let me explain: WIG is an acronym that stands for *W*ildly *I*mportant *G*oal.

So – how do you determine what your WIGs should be?

Well, as I've already told you, I like to ask questions – and here comes one of my favorite ones:

What's possible?

As an executive coach, I routinely ask my clients to share their goals with me, so I can see where they're at and where they want to be. That means I've had a chance to analyze the goals of hundreds of people over the years and really get a sense of how they all stack up as a whole. Now, keeping in mind these are the goals of smart, highly-functioning and ambitious people, what I'm about to say about their goals may surprise you.

Most of them don't aim too high and miss. In my opinion, most aim too low just to make sure they hit!

But let's be fair. I'd say 99% of us don't ask what's possible. Which is what makes that other 1% so extraordinary in comparison.

So here's another question - wouldn't you like to be extraordinary?

When you look back on your life, when you look at the times that made you feel the happiest and the most fulfilled, those times probably involved you meeting a big challenge successfully. That challenge may have involved a relationship, a work situation, a class in school, whatever – but it was most likely a difficult thing you accomplished, despite the odds, and that made you feel extremely satisfied with both yourself and how you had overcome the obstacles in your way.

A WIG should leave you with that feeling once you're reached it.

That's why I think WIGs are, indeed, wildly important.

When you set the bar a little above what you think you're capable of, you've hit on a true WIG – because it's a goal that's going to force you to grow beyond where you are and take you out of your comfort zone. You'll have to stretch to do something you ordinarily wouldn't think you could do.

It's about what's possible to do. *Not* something that you're certain you can do.

What's the point of a goal you're *certain* you can achieve? That's just complacency – and complacency kills. When you're sure you can get something done, there's no sense of a challenge or creating a new opportunity in certainty. There's no possibility of growing your skills, talents or abilities. There's only doing what you already know you can do.

That's not what goals are about. That's not what life is all about.

In 1961, President John F. Kennedy asked my favorite question. With the U.S. losing badly to the Soviets in the space race, he asked what was possible – and decided that putting a man on the moon was the answer. So JFK announced to Congress, the American people and the world that we would complete a moon landing by the end of the decade. Now, the President knew when he made that promise that there was no way that anybody could guarantee that something that fantastic could be done. The U.S. was very far from having the technology or the know-how to pull off a moon landing. But JFK figured, if he made the commitment, they'd have to figure out how to get it done. He thought it was *possible*.

And because he thought it was possible, NASA ended up doing it for real in July of 1969 – with five months to spare before we hit the '70's.

As you gain experience and knowledge, you develop an intuition for what's possible. You know what's difficult – but doable. Respect that intuition or you miss out on valuable opportunities. Look beyond today to two or three years down the line, even a decade like JFK did, and ask yourself what's possible for *you.*

That's where you'll find *your* WIGs.

With all that in mind, let's look at a few of the hairs you should weave into your WIGs.

WIG #1: Don't have too many goals.

I'm a big fan of simple as opposed to complicated, especially when it comes to goal-setting. Whether we're talking about one person or a huge organization, success comes from focusing on a few important things rather than trying to do everything at once. People like Steve Jobs believed that and so does Warren Buffet, who said, "I can't be involved in 50 or 75 things. That's a Noah's Ark way of investing – you end up with a zoo that way."

It's the same with goals. Goals are like chickens; when you're chasing 30 or 40 of them at the same time, you end up mostly chasing yourself. Focus on one or two of them at a time, however, and you'll make progress. It's the same with your goals. When you have a small number of WIGs in place (I suggest one to four), you're focused on what should get the most priority in your day-to-day life – and you act accordingly.

WIG #2: Be realistic.

I know, you're saying, "Ed, you just told me to shoot for the moon a page or two ago!" Yes, but I also said you should set your goals a *little* above your normal bar. I talk to people all day long about goals – and some common ideas that come up are being ambitious, being aggressive, thinking outside the box, and beginning with the end in mind. But you know what we never talk about?

Being ridiculous.

For example, what if I took the superhero theme of this book too seriously – and decided that, in three months, I was going to learn to fly (and without a plane!)? Well, in three months, when I would climb out on my roof ready to swoop over the trees of West Virginia, I had better hope that, after I jump into the air, there are some soft bushes underneath me for landing purposes. Because my landing would be very quick and very brutal.

The moral of this story? You may not be *sure* you can fulfill a WIG – but you have to be darn sure it's at least attainable.

WIG #3: There's no such thing as a free lunch.

I remember seeing an infomercial for an exercise machine, and it basically implied that you could work out 3 times a week, 20 minutes at a time, for 6 weeks and you'd end up looking amazing. I did the math – and realized what they were really saying was this: If you're sitting on the couch with 50 pounds to lose, you only need to do a total of 6 hours of exercise over a month and a half to end up looking like the 25-year-old swimsuit model that's in the infomercial. Well, that's nonsense – as are many other marketing claims that you can get rich quick, find love fast, and repair your credit in a month.

The truth is any worthwhile goal is going to require some real sweat. That means putting in a lot of work through a sustained effort over a long period of time. It just makes sense. If you want to create meaningful change in your relationships, your business, your finances, your fitness…well, it's going to be hard going at times. And there are going to be some speed bumps along the way – you just have to promise yourself that when you hit those bumps, you won't quit.

WIG #4: Aim for accountability.

Do you have a friend or loved one who's as into goals as you are? Make that person your accountability partner – and check in daily or weekly with them to make sure both of you are doing what you need to in order to reach your objectives. When you're acting alone, it's far too easy to let yourself off the hook – but when you know you might disappoint another person, it can give you that extra bit of motivation to get you past a rocky patch.

WIG #5: Let others inspire you - not bring you down.

It's fun to cruise the internet and see what goals other folks are setting and reaching. Feel free to take inspiration from them – but don't just simply copy them. Your goals should be about *you* - and customized to fit your situation. You're an original - the only "you" there is - so make sure your goals are equally unique. Others may think your goals are wrong for one reason or another – they may even feel they'll disrupt or threaten your relationships with them. Well, what ultimately matters is if your goals are right for you, not them.

WIG #6: Always, always write down your WIGS!

In my chapter about positive thinking, I talked about the importance of affirmations. Well, your WIGs should be a part of your affirmation process. That's why you should write them down and read them – out loud or to yourself – at least once every day. Feel free to continue to tweak them and modify them until you feel completely happy with them. And keep drumming them into your head until they're an integral part of who you are.

Why is this important? If you remember, in the last chapter, we talked about purpose – your "Why" and how it drives you forward. Well, think of your WIGs as your GPS to help you navigate your way during that drive. The more you plant those WIGs in your subconscious, the more automatically you'll function in service of those goals and the more they'll motivate you to achieve. You'll also be less likely to do anything that violates your WIGs – for example, you'll think twice about eating that donut if you want to lose weight. Instead, your WIGs will become second nature – and you'll find that you're almost on autopilot as you cruise on to where you want to go.

I realize that attempting to take on WIGS can be hairy for some people. But you'll find it's all worth it when you finally fulfill them. Best of all, when you've completed them, it's time to start all over again.

That's right – you get to flip your WIGs!

Feel free to groan.

SUPER SCORECARD #3

Superpower:	**Setting Wildly Important Goals**
Allows you to:	**Reach Objectives, Grow and Transform Your Life**
Obtained by:	**Effort and Accountability**
Arch Enemy:	**Complacency**

EAT YOUR OWN DOG FOOD: YOUR WALK TALKS AND YOUR TALK TALKS ... BUT YOUR WALK TALKS LOUDER THAN YOUR TALK TALKS!

Yes, the title of this chapter is "Eat Your Own Dog Food." Ready for some gourmet dining?

Well, lower your anxiety level, because I'm not actually advocating that you chow down on dog chow. It's actually a metaphor. For what? I'll get to that in a minute.

First, let's consider that least desired of all entrées, the lowly dog food. Of course, none of us who use only two legs to walk is all that anxious to dig into a big bowl of Alpo. That being said, if push came to shove, we *could* eat it. We could even live on it. But again, it's nothing we'd be gung-ho about, unless we were on a reality TV show and they were going to pay us a lot of money to do it (and I mean a LOT of money).

So, when I suggest you should eat your own dog food, I'm saying you need to do something a little unpleasant that's of your own making. You'll survive it, but it might not be the most fun you'll ever have in your life.

Now – let's unlock the metaphor and move on to the point. "Eat your own dog food" is really just another way to say, "Practice what you preach." You know, walk the talk and do as you say – because if there's one thing all of us human beings excel at, it's letting other people know *exactly* how they should live their lives. In our little metaphor, those kinds of moral pronouncements are, frankly, the dog food we all dish out. And we're very, very anxious to try and get others to eat it.

But when it comes down to us eating our own dog food? Well, *that* thought can be just as unappetizing as munching on an actual Milkbone. However, doing so is *crucial* to our self-development.

Here's why. One of the most important cornerstones of being a true leader is serving as a living example of the principles you claim to believe in. It's much more essential to consistently *act* according to your principles than it is to constantly *talk* about them – as people are more inspired by actions than they are by words. This is the essence of authentic leadership.

I've had many employees over the years, as well as hundreds of coaching clients in both one-one and group situations, and one of my consistent talking points to them is to stay in touch with their values and act accordingly. It's always something to strive for, even though nobody always bats a thousand. When you do strike out, however, it's a good reality check – and reinforces the importance of walking your talk.

If you're a parent, you've learned this lesson many times over. You might lecture your kids on cleaning up their room - but if they walk into your bedroom and can't see the floor because it's completely covered with your dirty clothes, how can they take you seriously? Worse, they're going to give themselves permission to continue to be slobs because you do. If you're a boss, the same dynamic can easily take place. Let's say you push your employees to work harder – then, later that day, they walk into your office and find you catching some z's on the couch. When that happens, you can expect a lot of eye-rolling behind your back every time you try to motivate them to be more productive.

A real leader shouldn't put him or herself in that situation. A real leader needs to be *better* than those who are followers.

Unfortunately, it turns out we're all human and sometimes not quite as diligent as we should be. I am not ashamed to confess that I regularly fall short of perfection – and I never will be. It is not about perfection .... It's about continuous improvement. And here's a good example of how I've thrown my own dog food out the window in the past.

For years, I've tried to teach my kids how to handle stressful situations – to keep their emotions under control and try to view things objectively without freaking out. I would tell them to, instead, and as calmly as possible, work through problems while keeping their priorities straight. I would add that I knew it wasn't possible to eliminate all anxiety, but it was certainly possible to get through trouble spots while keeping your cool. On one occasion, I was pretty proud of the wonderfully enlightening and instructional talk I had delivered to them along those lines – and I was pretty certain they would now be able to easily cope with all of life's ups and downs, thanks to my sage advice. Father knows best, you know.

So, a week or so later, how impressed do you think my kids were to see me acting all angry and irritable because *I* felt overextended and under pressure? Yeah, father knows best, but acts like the worst. My own dogfood? Yecch. Who wants to eat that garbage? Can I put in an order for a nice New York strip steak instead?

Well, sadly, no, I can't and I shouldn't order that steak. Instead, I had to recommit to practicing what I preach ....eating my own dog food, because, to be honest, when I do, I'm happy with the meal. After I'm done with my doggie dinner, after I've sucked it up and behaved as I should, I feel a whole lot better than if I hadn't. It sure beats slinking away sheepishly after a tantrum.

Eating your own dog food becomes more important the higher you ascend in life. That's because the more power you have, the easier it is to feel like the rules apply to everybody else but you. Heck, in the last fifty years we've seen one U.S. President resign and maybe a couple of others who should have, simply because they thought they were beyond the law. However, they're the ones who should represent it more than anybody else in our country.

Yes, even the president has to eat his own dog food.

John Maxwell, my mentor, put forth a very succinct and powerful three-point path to realize this goal: "Leaders know the way, show the way, but the most important thing to me is that they go the way."

Let's break down this very important thought to conclude this chapter.

Know the Way: You take yourself to a point where you understand what leadership is all about and how to inspire your own peak performance. This is purely about self-development, where you learn what's required of yourself to really stand out from the crowd.

Show the Way: Pedantic lecturing doesn't really cut it with most people; instead, you need to develop the communication skills to relate to people effectively. I'm talking about your kids, your employees, anybody who sees you in a leadership position. "Show the way" through humor, through relatable examples, through understandable concepts and people will appreciate the effort.

Go the Way: Yes, we're talking about eating that darn old dog food again. Again, if you just show the way to those around you, without actually *going* that way, you'll find yourself to be a fairly ineffectual leader.

Here's a way to really analyze how well you're practicing what you're preaching: Pretend someone has been making a video of all your activities during the day, like on an episode of the old sitcom, *The Office.* Would viewers be motivated by watching how you behave – or would they be snickering at you like they used to at Steve Carell on that program, a boss who regularly violated his own guidelines for his workers?

The answer is pretty clear: A leader shouldn't be leaving a laugh track in his or her wake.

SUPER SCORECARD #4

Superpower:	**Self-Leadership**
Allows you to:	**Gain Discipline and Direction, Inspire Others**
Obtained by:	**Careful Self-Monitoring**
Arch Enemy:	**Hypocrisy**

THE ULTIMATE SALES HERO

I know a dirty little secret about you.

Don't worry, I'm not going to spread it around your neighborhood or anything. This is between you and me. But we do have to talk about this and talk about it now.

Here's the secret: You're a salesperson.

"No, Ed, no," you're shouting at this book, "I'm not a salesperson! I'm not, I tell ya, I'm not!" Sure, sure, that's what they all say. People go around claiming they're students, teachers, accountants, receptionists, dentists, bus drivers, whatever. Anything but...*a salesperson!*[1]

Ugh.

Sorry, but sometimes the truth is ugly. And the truth is...you're a salesperson. And I can prove it.

When you were in high school and you had to do an oral book report, guess what? You had to *sell* that report in your delivery to the teacher and the rest of your class. If you're an office worker, there will come a point when you want to ask your bosses for a raise or a promotion – or talk with somebody else about hiring you for a completely different job, if you want to change careers. Once again – you have to *sell* them on the idea. Even a dentist has to *sell* his or her patients on a treatment they might need, so they can maintain good oral health.

And it doesn't stop there. Your personal life requires sales expertise as well. Suppose you're interested romantically in another person? You

---

1 By the way, I used to be a salesperson too. I'm only feigning disgust here. I'm a pretty good actor, huh?

have to sell them on the idea of dating you (and, by the way, my wife still thinks she got taken!). Or maybe your brother thinks he and his family should come stay with you for a month – you have to sell him on why it's absolutely a horrible plan! Even if you're four years old and you want your parents to buy you a candy bar, you *still* have to sell 'em on it. So, trust me, at some point during almost every day of your life – you have to be a salesperson!

The question now becomes – are you a good salesperson or a lousy one?

Those who can successfully sell others more often get what they want out of life. Those who lack this essential skill often don't - unless they have a truly outstanding skill or talent that gets them attention all on its own. But, as I've already noted earlier in this book, there are very few *truly* gifted people – which means the rest of us must rely on some level of salesmanship to advance our lives.

That's why you must embrace and nurture your inner salesperson.

As you may have guessed, this chapter is about selling. And, as you're probably aware, there have been about 20 billion words or so written on this subject ever since the very first sale in history, when a snake sold Adam and Eve a bill of goods. So you may think there's nothing new under the sun here – but please don't skip ahead to the next chapter just yet. I've taught professional selling at university level and I was in corporate sales and marketing for about 20 years, so I might just have some things to say on the subject you haven't heard before – including revealing the identity of the Ultimate Sales Hero.

See what I just did with that last part? I sold you on reading the rest of this. At least I hope I did!

First of all, I want to blow apart a couple of commonly-believed myths about selling.

Myth Number One: Extroverts make the best sales people. They're the ones with the firm handshakes, confident smiles and a smooth patter of conversation designed to immediately ingratiate themselves with their prospective buyer.

Myth Number Two: Introverts make the worst sales people. Those who are uncomfortable meeting and greeting people, who are a lot happier at home by themselves than they are with others, they just don't have the knack. If they can't make conversation, they can't make a sale, right?

Wrong - on both counts.

This isn't my personal opinion, by the way, this is science talking. A study published in *Psychological Science* in 2013[2] tracked over 300 salespeople on their rounds to see who did the best – and what personality traits they shared.

Conclusion? The extremely extroverted sales people had about the same percentage of successful sales calls as the extremely introverted. In other words – they sold *equally as well*.

A little shocked? Well, I was.

Now, here's the kicker - another personality type completely blows away both the introverts and the extroverts when it comes to selling. As a matter of fact, I call this person the Ultimate Sales Hero for good reason – because he is. And yet, you can find this particular superhero everywhere, among your family, friends and neighbors.

As a matter of fact, chances are good that you *are* one!

Ladies and gentlemen, let me introduce you to the Ambivert, a real-life superhero who combines the best of *both* introverted and extroverted characteristics – and whose mightiest of selling powers have been confirmed by the aforementioned *Psychological Science* study.

The Ambivert's effectiveness confirms something about human nature I've always considered to be true: In sales, as in so many other things in life, it's *moderation* that carries the day. You tilt too far one way or the other, and you risk upending whatever mission you're attempting. In this case, if you're too talkative, it can grate on people and cause them

2 Grant, Adam M. "Rethinking the Extraverted Sales Ideal," *Psychological Science* June 2013 vol. 24 no. 6

to think you're a phony who's trying too hard to make the sale. On the other hand, if you're too quiet, then they often don't know what to make of you – because you lack the ability to forge strong connections with people you don't know very well.

However, both problems are solved when you don the costume of the Ambivert. You know when to talk and make your point - and also when to lay back and listen. When you make your sales pitch, you can easily access the extroverted side of yourself. Then, when the prospect reacts to what you're saying, you can bring out your introvert, who is happy to focus on what the prospect is saying, allowing you to respond intelligently and respectfully to their thoughts and concerns. In the words of the author of the study, *"The Ambivert advantage stems from the tendency to be assertive and enthusiastic enough to persuade and close, but at the same time, listening carefully to customers and avoiding the appearance of being overly confident or excited."*

I'm a big Red Sox fan, so baseball is one of my favorite sports. And I know for a fact that a player who's ambidextrous is always going to have a tremendous advantage in the game. If he can bat well either right-handed or left-handed, he's got a lot more flexibility when facing specific pitchers. And if he can throw just as well with both hands, he's going to be an awesome asset when fielding. So it is with Ambiverts. The more comfortable you are with switching between your extrovert and introvert, the more powerfully you'll perform in your personal interactions.

The problem is the Ambivert's powers aren't recognized; instead, it's the extroverts who are traditionally seen as the sales superstars. But, if I can continue my baseball analogy, if you don't have your introvert in the on-deck circle ready to step up to the plate when needed, you'll strike out with what I consider to be one of the most crucial aspects of the sales process.

Don't get me wrong, there are a lot of important elements to selling, such as asking the right questions, targeting the right potential customers and so forth. But there's one underlying fundamental ability you absolutely *need* to have to really ensure successful selling, whether it's as a profession or just in your day-to-day life.

That ability is *empathy.*

You must legitimately *care* about the other person, whoever it is you're selling to, in order to succeed. If you don't, you can't effectively read the signals that person is putting out, nor will you be able to speak that person's language. You must start with a genuine concern for that person - or your efforts will all too easily fall apart.

And your introvert is who will do the heavy lifting when it comes to empathy. The introvert *wants* to connect on a deeper level. Your extrovert, in contrast, wants to keep pulling out arguments for why the other person should do what you want them to – it's all about technique. Well, that's important too, but it's superficial – and it's only about what *you* want.

The real secret to sales is giving the other party what *they* want. You identify that through empathy.

Let's say you're having a feud with a professional colleague. You want to sell the guy on a reconciliation, because it will make both your lives a little easier. So you go in and make your best case for why it would be in both your best interests if you shake hands and make up. For example, you tell him people get uncomfortable around the two of you and it makes both of you look bad. Or there are projects both of you could work on together that would give you both a business advantage.

Good reasons, sure, but the guy just keeps glaring at you – because all you're doing is trying to talk him into burying the hatchet without even addressing how the hatchet got there in the first place. By only trying to talk him into a papered-over truce, rather than directly addressing *why* he's been upset with you and how you can resolve it, he's most likely going to stay mad at you.

Now, imagine if you took a completely different approach. Imagine you went in to see him and just started the conversation as a heart-to-heart talk to resolve your differences, rather than a sales pitch about how you could both benefit from a reconciliation. It could all so easily go differently – and create a long-term solution that will leave both of you very satisfied with the outcome.

Empathy. It creates powerful lasting bonds that bring powerful lasting rewards for everyone involved – if we remember it's not about the short-term transaction, it's about the long-term relationship.

The late, great Dr. Stephen Covey, author of the mega-bestseller, *The Seven Habits of Highly Effective People*, listed as one of those seven habits, "Think win-win." That's exactly what I'm talking about – an outcome both parties feel is just and are happy with. Of course, many people don't buy that. They want to win and make the other person lose. To them, it's a dog-eat-dog world where it's every man for himself, so "Win – Lose" is their preferred result.

Well, when you take advantage of the other person to get what you want, it feels great at the moment – you got what you wanted. But in the long run? The other person is going to feel tricked, ripped-off and resentful. That person is going to complain to others in your circle about you. Soon, you have a bad reputation, and it becomes increasingly difficult to get anyone to trust you. Without that trust, it will become more and more difficult to talk anyone into anything.

That's why the "Win-Lose" approach frequently turns into a just plain "Lose" for the person who insists on using it.

Empathy ensures the "Win-Win." And your introvert delivers empathy.

But let's not leave your extrovert out in the cold – because we need that skill-set in the room too.

There's an endless debate in sales over what's more important – style or substance, the sizzle or the steak. Well, of course, they're both important. The steak is the substance, the facts of the matter at hand. If you're selling yourself, it's a matter of what your talents and skills are and what you can bring to the job. If you're selling a product, it's all about what that product can do for the person you want to buy it. The steak is all about what you're actually selling.

But it doesn't have that much to do with actually *selling*.

If you think that steak is all you need, you're going to run into some walls. You need the sizzle, you need the confidence and the enthusiasm that shows the other person you *truly believe in what you're selling*. If you can't show you have faith in what you're selling, then why should the other person have any? Why should anybody get excited about something that you don't seem to be excited about?

Of course, you can have the greatest sizzle in the world and a rotten steak. But, because you have that sensational sizzle, you might sell a few of those steaks. That, however, takes you into "Win – Lose" territory – which means you're not going to get many repeat customers. That's why you need a great steak and the sizzle to go with it. As I hope I've made clear, that sizzle doesn't mean you have to be flashy or phony. But it *does* mean you have to have a passion for your product. That's what ultimately attracts people to you and your business.

In conclusion, let us sing the praises of the Ambivert, the Ultimate Sales Hero…

The Ambivert, who can not only radiate an exciting super-spiel that knocks prospects off their feet, but also uses his incredible empathetic abilities to bond with others on a deep level that enables him to fully understand their needs! The Ambivert! He doesn't have to defeat Dr. Doom in a battle – he just talks him out of being such a creep!

The Ambivert! Not a member of the Avengers yet – but just you wait! Even that super group will need someone to negotiate their next movie deal!

SUPER SCORECARD #5

Superpower:	Salesmanship
Allows you to:	Increase Your Persuasion Power
Obtained by:	Being Empathetic, Genuine and Enthusiastic
Arch Enemy:	Underwhelming or Overbearing Personality

END OF THE BOOK

nd of the book? How can that be? There are still so many pages left –
are they just for doodling?

Don't despair, this isn't really the end of the book – this is just the
end of this particular *section* of the book. In the previous chapters, I've
tried to convey some important "mindset principles" that are best es-
tablished in the beginning of your life quest, rather than along the way.
These are the fundamentals that are designed to make all the rest of the
stuff a lot easier.

So why have I titled this chapter, "End of the Book"?

Because that's the name of one of my favorite mindset exercises, one
that can be of great use to anyone facing challenging circumstances or
entering an uncertain situation where the outcome matters a great deal
to you. Rather than approach these kinds of troublesome conditions
armed with nothing but a cold sweat, the "End of the Book" exercise can
be an excellent coping mechanism that will enable you to handle things
in the best way possible.

And isn't that the best way to end our exploration of mindset?

Here's how "End of the Book" works.

Let's say you buy a book, a suspense-thriller of the type James
Patterson writes. And let's say...well, you cheated. You can't help
yourself. You went and read the last twenty pages of the book to find
out how the plot got resolved. You see how all the mysteries are resolved, who the real bad guy was, and how the good guy managed to
defeat the whole conspiracy or master plan that was working against

him - everything the previous 320 pages was designed to build up to, you now know.

And *now* you go back to page 1 to start reading where you were supposed to.

However, as a reader, you will now have a completely different experience than if you hadn't read the last twenty pages. When you usually read these kinds of books, your pulse starts racing and you can't stand the suspense. Now, because you know how it all comes out...it's kind of relaxing. You don't get as scared or nervous every time one of the good guys is in jeopardy. Instead, you can carefully analyze how the author manipulates the plot and characters as you learn the whole story that led up to the ending you already read. It's much more interesting than nerve-wracking.

Well, guess what? You can have the same experience - with your life.

Let's say you are approaching a stressful meeting or conversation that you must have that's causing you to lose sleep. How do you eliminate that stress – so you can get through it as calmly and objectively as possible?

Simple. Read the end of the book.

In other words, *imagine* whatever it is you're worried about coming out the way you want it to. "Read" how it gets resolved in a positive and vivid manner. If you'd rather, picture it like a movie rather than as a book and "see" how it all actually plays out. Go through the entire interaction you're dreading. See yourself performing flawlessly. Watch the other person or people challenging you and go through how you'll respond in an articulate and eloquent way. And find out how you re-solve everything to everyone's satisfaction, including your own. Use your powers of imagination and visualization.

And once you thoroughly understand the "End of the Book," then keep rereading it in your head before you need to go through the situation for real. Then, when that time does come, you'll find yourself calmer, cooler, and confident as you navigate the real interaction. Your practice will help you to perform at your best.

And that's it.

Now, does doing this exercise guarantee that you'll get your way? Does it in any way promise you'll be happy with the outcome? The answer is no – that's a kind of magic I haven't really come across yet.

What this exercise *does* promise, however, is that you'll walk into the situation as prepared as possible and ready to perform at your peak. This is an amplification of what we discussed in the positive thinking chapter, "On Becoming," when we talked about doing everything you can mentally to create the outcomes you want to see. When you successfully bring the "End of the Book" to life in your head, much of your stress and nervousness will be alleviated, allowing you to avoid getting in a sweat and saying the wrong thing due to nervousness.

That's as good as you can get before you enter troubled waters. And if I were you, I'd take it!

SUPER SCORECARD #6

Superpower:	**Positive Visualization**
Allows you to:	**See Pathways to Success**
Obtained by:	**Imagining Your Preferred Outcome**
Arch Enemy:	**Anxiety**

PART 2
ATTAINING YOUR POWERS:
TRAINING FOR TRIUMPH

> *"I learned the value of hard work by working hard."*
> – MARGARET MEAD

"*I gotta go to work.*"

That's what Michael Keaton told Kim Basinger in the 1989 version of *Batman* when she made a romantic pass at him. And if I remember correctly what Kim looked like in 1989, that's some willpower.

Hopefully, you've developed that kind of willpower from reading the first section of this book. Now, it's time to apply your new supersized mindset to how you actually live your life: That means acquiring some more "powers" that will aid you in your endless fight against such bad traits as disorganization, sloppy work and giving up on goals.

Even superheroes have to master their craft. Superman had to learn how to fly without randomly crashing into mountains, Iron Man had to master being in his souped-up metal suit, and Batman, of course, had to train 24/7 to get himself in peak shape. We're no different – we have to take the basic talents and abilities we were born with and apply them diligently in our lives to become the best versions of ourselves.

To that end, in this section of the book, I'll be sharing some of my secrets that will help you perform at a higher level, achieve more objectives and live a happier, more productive life. I will warn you – you're going to encounter a lot of alphabet soup in this section of the book. I'll be talking about D's and V's as well as some ABC's – because I've found that spelling out precepts in this manner provides a memorable way to retain information simply and effectively.

So get ready, superhero – because it's time to spring into action. Turn the page ASAP – and you'll get some valuable life advice PDQ!

THE FOUR C'S OF PRODUCTIVITY

Plan your work. Work your plan.

That's one of my favorite sayings. Here's why: It begins with the three little words, "Plan your work," which is all about thinking through what you want to do - and then reverse-engineers them to remind you those thoughts need a real-life application if they're going to mean anything.

Thinking and doing. One without the other doesn't get you very far.

We've all met people who continually talk about all their grand plans for the future. You run into them a year or so later, and they're still talking about the exact same plans – without having done one single thing to move them forward since you saw them last.

Why? Hard to say.

Maybe because, in their heads, they've already repeatedly accomplished what they wanted to accomplish so many times, they're bored with it!

On the flip side, we've also all met people who are perpetual motion machines with no perceivable purpose. They keep incredibly busy but don't actually advance their lives despite all their constant activity. Maybe they're in a constant social whirl with friends, spending hours cooking extravagant meals, or locked in endless video game battles against people halfway around the world on the same online network. There's no question you can lose yourself in the internet for very long periods of time – but there's a reason they call online activity "virtual." And that's because it's NOT REAL.

Plan your work. Work your plan. Reality is important and so is your commitment to changing yours. When you create a state of mind where you can encourage your own productivity on an ongoing basis, you'll be amazed at the goal-reaching ground you'll cover.

Here are my 4 C's that can help you set the stage to get real-world stuff done in a way that brings results and makes you feel great about how you spend your time:

C #1: Choice

Granted, some life-changing events aren't your choice. The death of a loved one, an incapacitating accident, an expensive tax bill you didn't expect – all of these unexpected events can delay your progress in life.

In most cases, however, most of your life circumstances do directly result from your decisions. Some of those decisions have immediate repercussions (you don't prepare for an important meeting and things don't go your way), some of them are long-range (you dropped out of college and are repeatedly turned down for quality jobs because you don't have the required degree).

That's why you've got to own the choices you make and not blame others for where those choices have taken you. When you don't take that kind of personal responsibility, you don't spend a lot of time on making sure your choices are the right ones. And you end up repeating easily-avoided mistakes that will continue to haunt you in the future. However, when you *do* recognize that your choices have real consequences, you're a lot more careful about making them.

How to Put This "C" into Action: Be conscious of the choices you make throughout the day. Understand that any time you choose *not* to do what you need to do, you're stopping your momentum in its tracks. And be aware that, at any given time, you can stop yourself and say, "Where I am, how I'm thinking, how I'm feeling, how I'm responding to the world is in *my* power to choose."

C #2: Certainty

The best way to be productive in a targeted and effective manner is to have a clear understanding of where you're going, how your strengths can help you get there and why you want to go there. When you develop this kind of certainty for yourself, you'll always have a sense of whether one of your choices is taking you in the right direction – or the wrong one.

Confusion is often debilitating; you can spend way too much time and energy trying to sort things out when you don't develop certainty. Don't get me wrong, some confusion is inevitable when you're trying to determine your path – but once you have determined it, certainty should be your constant companion.

How to Put This "C" into Action: Create an overall life direction for yourself that you feel excited and enthusiastic about – and that matches both your abilities and aspirations.

C #3: Clarity

Certainty leads to our third "C," which is *Clarity*. Clarity implies you have a clear vision of where you're going and how to get there – and that requires a vital part of the productivity process, *planning*. When you plan carefully how to reach the next level in your life path, you should be able to then visualize how to succeed with that plan - it's a little like my "End of the Book" exercise from the last chapter, but on a much grander scale.

Clarity will help you when you feel overwhelmed, even helpless, because of what you've chosen to undertake. It happens – especially when you set the bar high. When you do feel that way, stop and try to recapture your original clarity of purpose to figure out what your next move should be. Take the time to get yourself back on track so that you take your great intentions and turn them into real results - by directing your productivity towards the right ends.

How to Put This "C" into Action: Visualize your plans until you have a clear vision of how to fulfill them – and refer back to that clarity when you lose focus.

C #4: Courage

First of all, let me say my 4 C's are like my kids – I love 'em all. But having said that…this one I maybe love a little more than the others.

Why? Well, maybe it goes back to the old saying, "The best laid plans of mice and men often go awry" – or, as Robert Burns' original Scottish version has it, "gang aft agly" (best read with authentic burr, by the way). In other words, at some point, no matter how carefully you plot out your moves, some plans will still "gang agly," because that's life. And sometimes life has a very different idea of how things should go than you do.

That's when a big dose of courage comes in handy.

Without that courage, it's easy to get *dis*couraged. It's easy to lose your game, forget the plot, and get down and depressed. You might even feel tempted to give up on a difficult dream and settle for a lesser one.

When that happens, hit the reset button. Revisit the first 3 C's and regain your vision and determination. Then use that fourth C, courage, to face your current failure or difficulty and analyze as objectively as possible whether it really affects your bigger game plan …or is, more likely, just a temporary setback.

Fear is a normal human reaction to trouble. Overcoming fear is how great things get done. Courage is the C we all need when we're no longer sure how to get from point A to point B, but we still are certain we have to keep going forward. That's why I love this "C" – and you should learn to love it too!

How to Put This "C" into Action: Be strong and remember your original vision – and also know most setbacks are temporary. So keep going. Because if you don't keep moving towards your goal…well, you'll never get there!

SUPER SCORECARD #7

Superpower:	Productivity
Allows you to:	Be More Efficient, Get More Done
Obtained by:	The 4 C's
Arch Enemy:	Apathy

THE ABC'S OF PERFORMANCE MANAGEMENT

If you really want to be super-successful – you first have to learn your ABC's. And appropriately enough, I learned my ABC's from a teacher.

This teacher happens to be an educator who works with children with learning issues – those who are called "special needs students." Of course, this can be a challenging occupation – and this particular teacher has found success using an "ABC" method to track and improve these students' academic performance.

Here's what these ABC's stand for:

Antecedent – the event or activity that immediately precedes a certain behavior.
Behavior – the actual behavior of the student that's observed.
Consequence – the event that immediately follows as a result of the behavior.

And here's an example of how this "ABC" chain works.

Let's say our *antecedent* is a student who is supposed to be working on an assignment is making nonsensical doodles on the paper instead – and the teacher tells the student to do what he is supposed to be doing. Let's say the *behavior* that results is that this particular student angrily throws a pencil at the teacher. The *consequence* is that the student is then either sent home for the day or must go to the principal's office.

If this pattern is repeated on different occasions, the question becomes, why does the student sometimes erupt in anger doing an assignment –

and, on other occasions, quietly does the work to the best of his ability? To find the answer, the teacher must focus on the antecedents to try and determine which produced a positive outcome – and which produced a negative one.

It may be that the student's anger erupts every time he's given an assignment he feels he doesn't have the ability to do correctly. Or it may just be having to do it in class, in front of other people, where he feels like he's being judged or won't be able to keep up with the rest of the class.

The point is, you don't know what's behind a positive or negative result unless you *examine* what preceded it. And this isn't a rule that's limited to the schoolroom. It's a rule I apply to business and personal performance management.

The big mistake many business people make is focusing simply on the behavior and the outcome. For example, a salesperson slinks back into the office complaining that he couldn't close a deal. He says he lost his focus in the middle of the pitch and he has to make sure not to do that again.

But it happens again. And again.

The real problem lies in what happened *before* the salesperson went on those unsuccessful calls. Maybe he didn't eat breakfast. Maybe he stayed up too late the night before. Whatever the reason, it had a physical effect on his performance on those particular days that he couldn't mentally shake.

So, the next time you find yourself flaming out in a business situation, don't just say to yourself, "I'll never do *that* again." Instead, find out why you *did* do it in the first place. Conversely, the next time you find yourself excelling, don't just assume you're suddenly an unstoppable force. Examine what circumstances might have helped you score on that occasion (and, no, sorry, you can't just say it was because you wore your lucky socks – try to stick to reality!).

Remember, it's the ABC's, not the BC's. That means you should never just look at the "B" (your behavior) or the "C" (the consequence of that behavior) – instead, dig into the "A" and work to understand your antecedent, so you know exactly what triggered "B" and "C."

At worst, you'll discover some important clues or potential opportunities to make positive changes. At best – you'll discover winning formulas you can replicate and revisit to create a pattern of solid performance.

And that, my friends, is the secret of why a superhero never loses a battle.

SUPER SCORECARD #8

Superpower:	Consistency
Allows you to:	Obtain Predictably Positive Results
Obtained by:	The ABC's of Performance Management
Arch Enemy:	Negative Patterns

WHAT'S SO HARD ABOUT TAKING
TWO MILLION FOOTSTEPS?

I'm sure many of you reading this are aware of the ancient Chinese philosopher Lao Tzu's iconic quote, "The journey of a thousand miles begins with one step."

Now, of course, this quote really doesn't refer to a physical journey – it's a metaphor for when you want to achieve a great and important goal. To reach such a goal, you have to "travel" a long way – and, as with any trip of substantial distance, you need to make the proper preparations. And those preparations need to be made before you even take that first step.

With that in mind, here some important things to consider while you're getting ready to go on your own personal thousand-mile "journey."

To begin with, I strongly believe that you should have an *expressed intention* to accomplish your goal, whether that goal is in your professional or personal life.

You might respond to that by saying, "Well, naturally, I have an intention to accomplish my goal, otherwise the goal wouldn't be there in the first place. You can't have a goal without an intention, right?"

Fair enough, but there's an extra word I put in my statement that also needs to be addressed – expressed. In other words, it's not enough that *you* know your intention – you need to let others know as well.

That means you have to verbalize your intentions to others besides yourself. Whether you do that through speaking to someone else either in person or on a phone call - or in a written form such as in an email – is up to you. The point is, the more you concretely put your intentions out there, the more likely it is that you will actually reach your goal.

Why's that? Two reasons.

Reason #1: Every time you *do* verbalize your intentions, you're not just telling others, you're also reinforcing that goal with yourself. In the process, you keep bringing that goal to the forefront of your own thoughts; making it top-of-mind will keep you working on how you can reach your goal and what your next steps should be.

Reason #2: You're recruiting accountability partners. Whoever you talk about your goal with is someone you're bringing along on your quest to achieve your objective. That's why you should be extremely *careful* about who you share your goal with. What you want is someone who will engage in what I call "benevolent accountability" – encouraging you and advising you in a positive manner. You don't need someone nagging you or busting your chops about what you have and haven't accomplished – no, you want somebody on *your* side to tell you the truth, but to do it in the nicest way possible.

So choose wisely – pick people who aren't abusive or abrasive, people you can trust not to hold your goals against you or somehow take advantage of this knowledge if your relationship with them goes wrong for some reason. You want someone you're entirely comfortable with, someone you know wants you to succeed and genuinely wants to help you on your way.

Expressed intention and benevolent accountability - a powerful combination to have in place as you start your journey towards your goal.

Another thing to do before you begin your thousand-mile journey to your goal? Take your temperature.

You can put away the thermometer - I'm not a doctor, nor do I play one on television. When I talk about temperature, I'm not talking about your body heat – I'm talking about your emotional heat.

As an executive business coach, I get asked frequently, "What kind of business people are the most successful? The ones who are fired up with passion – or the ones who remain calm in the heat of the moment?"

My answer? Both.

I respond that way not because I'm wishy-washy – but because I believe it's the right answer. To reach your goals and to be successful means you have to both run hot – *and* be cool.

Let's examine both of those temperatures.

By "run hot," I mean to say that you take yourself, your career, your clients and your business very seriously. You're connected to the "Why" we spoke of in the "Power of Purpose" chapter earlier in this book and that in turn fuels your passion and your drive to achieve.

But, at the same time, you have to "be cool" – or you'll burn yourself out, not to mention exhaust the people around you.

Have you ever been around someone who's always "on" – someone who always seems over-enthusiastic and can't relax? More than a little scary, right? It's much more reassuring – and motivating – to be around someone who has an authentic plan to succeed, but, at the same time, knows how to loosen up and enjoy a moment. So be that someone. Retain your sense of humor, as well as your humanity, and you'll attract a lot more people to your cause. And you'll also find it's a lot healthier way to live your life.

The great classic performers – I'm thinking of people like Cary Grant, Gene Kelly, Judy Garland, and Dean Martin – always made what they were doing on stage and screen look easy. They smiled so brightly and moved so naturally that it seemed like what they were doing was the easiest thing in the world. The best politicians – from John F. Kennedy to Ronald Reagan – had the same quality. The reality is these all-timers worked their butts off to make sure they could deliver that level of performance, a performance so powerful that I'm still referencing them decades later. These legends always kept the heat on their insides – and kept themselves cool on the outside. They ran hot and still were cool.

Do likewise and nobody will be lukewarm about your chances for success.

Now, let's return to the notion of using a journey of a thousand miles as a metaphor for your efforts to reach a big goal.

I've done the math (well, the calculator in my phone did, at least). Walking just one mile takes an average of about 2200 footsteps. A thousand miles? Now we're talking about over two million footsteps. Better have some comfortable shoes, right?

More importantly, you'd better know how to pace yourself during that long walk.

Quite often, those who want to perform at a much higher level want to do everything at once to make that happen. This is especially true with those who have a true leadership mentality – they're impatient and want to leapfrog to the end of their goal-driven journey without walking all those steps. You can't blame them – who wants to deal with two million-plus footsteps?

But seriously, when you try to skip all the little steps that go towards reaching a big goal, when you try to make each stride towards that goal enormous rather than manageable... Well, you're going to end up intimidated, discouraged or prematurely admitting defeat - three very undesirable destinations for the trip you're taking. It's a lot like a guy who has a goal of bench-pressing 500 pounds – and, at the moment, can barely get 100 up in the air. If he immediately tries to lift that 500 – well, the screams of pain will not only be heard in that gym, but in every other one within a 10 mile radius.

Big results come from small changes. When you put into effect the right little alterations to your usual patterns, you'll find yourself eventually creating huge outcomes that will blow you away. But...you have to be patient until they happen!

Here are four real-world examples of little things that will in time mean a lot...

1) Listening without interrupting.

Many people in leadership positions (senior managers, C-level executives, business owners) believe in talking first and listening later. When they want to set a goal for the business, their agenda is to dictate to everybody under them how they're going to achieve that specific objective.

First problem with that approach: If the leader doesn't get feedback on from the people who are at least partly responsible for achieving that goal, he or she is missing out on valuable on-the-ground information that could tremendously help or hinder progress.

Second problem: When the leader doesn't listen to anyone else, it discourages open communication and degrades the quality of relationships with and respect from the workforce. That, in turn, weakens their overall motivation to achieve the goal in question.

So let's be real – it's not all that hard to listen without interrupting. And it's amazing how big an advantage can be gained by doing something that easy to pull off. All it takes is the willpower to keep quiet for a few minutes and give someone else the floor.

2) Following up.

Whatever your business happens to be, if you don't follow up with clients and prospects, you're probably leaving a lot of money on the table.

And again, it's an easy thing to do. An email, a text, or a quick phone call can often jolt a reluctant party into revealing why they're hesitant to do a deal - or uncover a silly misunderstanding that's easy to clear up. Even just keeping in touch about a specific order or lingering issue will show your clientele that you're on top of things and you care about the relationship.

So set aside a few minutes of your day for simple follow-up messages. You'll realize better results over the long haul.

3) Eliminating temptation.

Sometimes the phrase "out of sight, out of mind" can be a big benefit to your efforts.

When you really know yourself, you know your weaknesses. You know what can easily pull you off the path to a goal and, instead, create an unwelcome setback that causes you to lose ground rather than gain it.

When possible, simply get rid of those temptations. Get them out of sight.

For example, maybe you're trying to get fit - exercise more, eat less junk, the usual routine. Well, take a look at what's in your pantry. What's unhealthy in there – and, even worse, currently calling to you to shove it in your mouth? Chocolate bars? Potato chips? Soda? Whatever it is, stop buying it and keep it from coming into your house or office.

Maybe a TV in your bedroom is preventing you from doing the reading you've been anxious to tackle, but, instead, you've been too distracted by ESPN, HGTV or whatever the cable channel letters are that haunt you on a nightly basis. Go ahead and take the TV out – remove the distraction and you'll do what's needed to achieve your goals.

Whatever's stopping you from doing what you should be doing to achieve what you're after, eliminate it from the picture if you find your willpower flagging on a regular basis. Sure, it's kind of a cheat – but "Whatever works," as a great man (not Lao Tzu, I'm pretty sure) once said.

4) Schedule a nightly planning session.

This is one of my personal favorites. When you spend a few minutes every evening either creating a plan for the next day or reviewing an existing one, you can make sure whatever you're doing is in alignment with whatever your highest priorities are. This is especially helpful if you're engaged in a long-term commitment to a goal, because you'll be able to make sure you make the amount of progress you're after on a regular basis.

This kind of planning session doesn't take a lot of time to do, but, oh, what a difference it makes.

The above are just my specific suggestions – I'm sure you can come up with some of your own. Just consider what little changes you can incorporate in your daily routine that will eventually make a big difference in your life. A lot can happen while you're taking those two million footsteps – so make yours a productive walk!

SUPER SCORECARD #9

Superpower:	**Goal Attainment**
Allows you to:	**Create Meaningful Change**
Obtained by:	**Long-term Planning and Execution**
Arch Enemy:	**Impatience**

THE 4 PILLARS OF PHYSICAL FITNESS

Imagine a superhero who decided to change his daily routine – and, instead of fighting crime and alien invasions, instead binge-watched Netflix shows for hours at a time, while he lounged on a couch and emptied a few bags of Doritos and a six-pack of Mountain Dew.

The next time that super-guy tried to fly, he might find his now-huge belly had become his biggest arch-enemy.

So far in this book, we've talked a lot about the need to create a powerful mindset. But we also have to remember that our brains are held hostage by our bodies – when bad things happen to your overall health, it can't help but affect your mental state. Willpower shrivels, distractions loom larger and the memory often stalls and sputters when we're out of shape and feeling ill.

A *true* superhero, of course, has to stay fit. With that in mind, let me reveal what I believe to be the Four Pillars of Physical Fitness.

(Right after I provide a disclaimer. I'm not a medical doctor, a personal trainer, nor am I a professional nutritionist. Before you undertake any exercise program or change in diet, consult a medical professional, especially if you're on any prescription drugs or have any other ongoing health issue.)

Pillar #1: Nutrition

Try putting diesel fuel in a car that doesn't run on it. Try putting regular gas in a car that requires premium. In both cases, you're driving towards disaster, as your vehicle will at some point show extreme displeasure at your ill-considered decision and pay you back by breaking down.

Every machine and every living being requires the *right* fuel to run efficiently. If you want to accomplish great things, you must feed your body with the right foods – or you simply won't have the energy to achieve at a high level.

When in doubt, avoid processed foods as much as you can. If you look at the ingredients on a package and you see a laundry list of compounds your uncle the nuclear scientist couldn't pronounce, you might want to quietly put that package back on the supermarket shelf. If an apple had an ingredient list, guess what would be on it? That's right – just "Apple."

So eat lots of fresh fruits and vegetables. Avoid chemicals and drugs like caffeine. As for meat, I know for years you've heard the commercials that say, "Beef. It's what's for dinner." Well, the occasional dinner is okay, but certainly not *every* dinner. In general, think about eating a lot more protein and a lot less carbohydrates and fat.

If you really feel your diet needs to change, keep a log of what you're eating. Examine problem areas and eliminate the bad foods that are either empty calories or harmful ones – you probably already know what they are. Replace those bad foods with things that are good for you as well as things you *like*. Yes, a Snickers bar can seem a lot more tempting than a banana – but think beyond that minute of pleasure to a lifetime of good health.

The sad fact is that two-thirds of Americans are overweight or even obese. Fighting that trend starts with what you yourself are eating on a daily basis.

Pillar #2: Water

Virtually every fitness expert will tell you – *drink more water*. Hydration is incredibly important and you should be downing eight to ten glasses of good old H_2O every day. You don't have to drink bottled water if the tap water is good in your area. It is in mine and that's what I drink.

And just so you know, coffee doesn't count and neither does soda – they're not substitutes. Just plain water and a lot of it. Okay, you'll visit the bathroom a little more often than you're used to – but just think of it as getting a few extra breaks during the day!

Pillar #3: Rest

Every morning, I post what I believe to be an inspirational quote on Facebook. And I do it at around 5 am most days. That freaks my fabulous Facebook friends (say that fast three times) to no end. They want to know, "Ed – how do you get up so early?" And I answer – "Because I go to bed so early!"

Don't misunderstand me, I'm not telling you to race the sun to see who can get up in the morning first like I do. What I am saying is the time between when you go to bed and when you get up needs to be enough time for you to wake up feeling refreshed and rested. In most cases, that amount of time should be around seven or eight hours.

An overwhelming number of studies show that Americans, in addition to being overweight, simply don't get enough sleep (and some studies actually link the two conditions). I know it can be hard to catch all forty winks, especially if you're trying to be a parent, a spouse *and* work a demanding job. Nevertheless, carving out enough time for sleep is crucial over the long run.

If you just can't swing it, I do know people who rely on power naps during the day to make up for their lack of nighttime sleep. Give it a try if it's an option.

Pillar #4: Exercise

This is a pretty obvious pillar of physical fitness – and the one most people shy away from. The thing is, you don't have to engage in a demanding and extreme regimen, such as Cross fit or, my personal favorite, P90X. Just make sure you're active on a regular basis, however that happens. For example, we got a dog a couple of years ago and, like any pooch, she needs to be walked quite often. That's a great form of exercise and one you can't avoid (unless you want your dog to decorate the living room rug on a daily basis).

Try to exercise for an hour, two to four times a week at least. Try to get your heart rate up every day if you can, it's good to give it a workout. One of those Fitbit devices can be a wonderful way to keep track of how much you're doing every day. It's also helpful if you have the room and the budget to put some exercise equipment in the house – it makes exercising a lot more convenient. We have a treadmill and an elliptical machine in our home; that way, when the weather is bad, we can still get a workout in.

Here's the bottom line – the body you're in is the only one you're going to get, unless you have a good friend with the last name of Frankenstein. So take care of it – and it will take care of you.

SUPER SCORECARD #10

Superpower:	**Physical Fitness**
Allows you to:	**Stay Healthy and Energetic**
Obtained by:	**Exercise, Proper Diet and Rest**
Arch Enemy:	**Inactivity and Bad Eating Habits**

THE CVD'S AND THE B'S: KEYS TO POWERFUL PRESENTATIONS

You've probably heard of TED talks. They're those mega-popular speeches where experts of all stripes dazzle you with their delivery as they explain an exhilarating idea in 18 minutes or less.

Well, when it comes to making a presentation to a crowd, everyone wants to have that kind of impact. The TED talk is the gold standard, in most people's minds. Unfortunately, many presentations are more dead than TED.

And to be honest, even some TED talks don't set the world on fire. Ever see the one where that guy takes three minutes to teach you how to tie your shoes correctly? (Not kidding – Google "worst TED talk ever" – and you'll come across it quickly!).

It's all too easy to create a presentation that's about as exciting as watching paint dry. I've seen them – and, to be brutally honest, I've even been guilty of delivering them! After being exposed to hundreds, even thousands, of these kinds of speeches, I have definitely witnessed the Good, the Bad and the Ugly – and I've learned some valuable lessons along the way, lessons I'd like to share with you in this chapter. Like anything else, when you master the basics of presenting, you can more often than not be a very effective speaker.

To my mind, there are three essential ingredients that must be right for a great presentation – what I call the "CVD" of a talk. And here they are:

1. Content

Content, as they say, is king. If you're talking about something that you can't make relevant to your audience – or that ultimately doesn't have a point – you're going to lose the crowd, guaranteed. So understand just who you're going to be talking to and decide how your subject relates to them – it's very important to make that connection as fast as you're able.

Also, always know where you want to end up – ask yourself, "What do I most want the audience to walk away thinking about?" Begin with that end in mind and work relentlessly towards it. Establish your point, make your point, prove your point and then demonstrate why the crowd needs to understand that point.

Don't take your audience down useless detours. Focus on what the audience needs to hear in regards to your subject, not on what you personally want to say. Stay off the soapbox: Self-indulgence doesn't go far on stage. It needs to be about them, not you.

Finally, less is more. Don't be repetitive and don't include a lot of fluff. Trust your audience – if you're clear and focused, they'll *get* it, without you having to hammer it home.

2. Visuals

There's an old expression, "Show, don't tell." And here's another one: "A picture is worth a thousand words."

Both of those well-worn axioms make the important point that visuals can make more of an impact than just the written word on its own. Visuals always make any presentation more palatable as well as more powerful – the right photo or illustration can instantly deliver a big idea in more effective a manner than pages and pages of written analysis. And that's why almost every internet article you click on will have video or pictures accompanying it.

People like to see visuals and so do I. That's why I'm a huge fan of using as many images as possible – it's one of the reasons I like to make video blogs instead of written ones. The fact is many people are better at learning through visuals rather than written material. And they find it more interesting to look at images or video than to just watch you talk (nothing personal – I'm sure you're easy on the eyes!).

These days, we live in a multimedia world – so shouldn't you have a multimedia presentation?

3. Delivery

There's no question that your content is crucial. But there's also an incredible amount of validity to the phrase, "It's not what you say, it's how you say it." When you deliver your material with energy, enthusiasm and passion, people are going to listen to you. They're going to be intrigued about what you're so excited about – because, who knows, they might get as excited about it as you are!

On the other hand, you could have the greatest content possible – maybe you just came up with the ultimate answer for world peace. However, if you deliver it in a dull, flat monotone, you might as well be that guy describing how to tie your shoes. If you don't seem interested in what you're talking about, if you don't demonstrate the relevance and importance in your delivery – how can you expect your audience to feel your topic is relevant or important?

People will remember how you made them *feel* long after they'll remember what you *said*. You may not like that, but it's the truth – and it's why you should always work on your performance as well as your content, especially if you're looking to raise your professional profile or be an effective communicator within a select group. If you deliver your content with passion and enthusiasm, you'll get a much better reception from your audience, and their enjoyment will be contagious. That in turn will lead to great word-of-mouth about your talents as a speaker.

Content, Visuals and Delivery – when you get all three of those right, you'll be a stage sensation.

Now, let's narrow the focus – to in-the-room presentations to VIP's.

I learned a lesson about 20 years ago and it still holds very, very true. As a matter of fact, it's my rule of thumb whenever I need to talk to a high-level executive or busy business owner – in other words, a Very Important Person whose time you dare not waste. We all have some of those in our lives and there are always times when we need a minute or two with them.

Here's the lesson – with VIP's, use the 3 B's.

The first B is be brilliant. You want to have all the facts at your fingertips of whatever it is you're seeing this person about, you want to be prepared to deliver your message in the best way possible, and, if you're bringing in a problem, you want to have a few options for how it gets solved.

The second B? Be sure to be brief. Don't tell a long story about what you had for breakfast that day, instead, bullet-point the information he or she needs to hear without a lot of extraneous info. Cut to the chase. Tell them what the situation is, ask them for what you want, find out what they want you to do. Brief!

And the last B? Be gone! Get up, if you've even taken the time to sit down, and leave the room.

The three B's for VIP's. Be brilliant, be brief and be gone. And that's all there is to it.

Although you do have the option to add a couple more B's to the equation when you're on your way out the door…

"Bye-bye."

SUPER SCORECARD #11

Superpower:	**Skilled Presenter**
Allows you to:	**Communicate Effectively**
Obtained by:	**Understanding How to Connect with People**
Arch Enemy:	**Lack of Preparation**

BELIEVING IS SEEING: LESSONS FROM THE WIZARD

The businessman was in dire straits.

He was deeply in debt, not making any sales and under tremendous pressure. Would he have to declare bankruptcy? How would he support his family if his company went completely under?

How bad would things get?

That was the question that plagued him night and day.

At the end of this particular workday, he felt too agitated to simply go home – so he took a walk in the park to try and think things through again, for the ten millionth time. Unfortunately, once again, he experienced no miraculous brainstorms. Feeling more defeated than ever, he finally sat down on a bench and buried his head in his hands.

It was at that moment that an elderly man approached him.

"What's wrong, son?"

After a few moments of small talk, the businessmen, for some reason, ended up pouring his heart out to the old man. Maybe it was because the senior was a stranger – there was nothing to lose in telling him everything. So the businessman did. He described how, despite being a fundamentally sound business, his company was on the verge of collapse. How a series of bad breaks was about to destroy everything he had worked for over the past 20 years. How he had no idea how to bring it back to financial health.

The old man, sitting next to him, listened carefully. He did not interrupt, he merely nodded and signaled that he wanted the businessman to keep talking – and when he was done, the old man reached into his coat pocket and pulled out a checkbook.

The businessman watched with a questioning look as the elderly gentleman wrote on one of the checks with a shaky hand, ripped it out of the checkbook and handed it over to the businessman. "Meet me here in a year so you can pay me back," said the old man abruptly and walked away without another word.

The businessman looked at the check in his hand. It was made out to "Cash" for a total of $500,000. And it was endorsed by John D. Rockefeller, who at the time, was the wealthiest man in the world.

Obviously, he had picked the right time to go for a walk in the park.

The dark cloud lifted from his mental state. This was exactly what he needed to get things back on track. He checked his watch to see if he could make it over to the bank before it closed and cash the check.

But then he stopped. Maybe he didn't need that money right this moment. Maybe he should put it in the safe at his office and just enjoy the security of knowing that cash was there in case he absolutely did need it. With that check in the safe, he didn't have to suffer sleepless nights or waste his energy on doomsday scenarios. He could just calmly and coolly analyze his various crises and try to work through them.

With a renewed sense of enthusiasm and confidence, he went back to his office and worked into the night. Over the next few weeks, he made arrangements with his creditors to delay or reduce immediate payments that were due. He also renewed his sales efforts and landed several large new contracts. He didn't forget his loyal employees, who had caught his funk and also felt doomed; he told them that he had a short term loan that would guarantee their viability and safeguard their jobs. Their morale also skyrocketed and they worked hard than ever to rebuild the business.

A year went by. Things completely turned around for the businessman. He anxiously returned to the park with the uncashed check from his safe so he could happily return it to Mr. Rockefeller and tell him how it inspired him to approach his situation in a positive and pro-active manner.

He turned a corner in the park - and there he was. The elderly man was sitting on the bench where the businessman had poured out his troubles exactly one year before. The businessman rushed up to him with a big excited grin.

But before he could say a word, a nurse came running up to the bench from the opposite direction and got to the old man first. She pulled him up on his feet.

"Is he all right?" asked the businessman. "I need to talk to him."

"Oh," responded the nurse. "I'm sorry, he really shouldn't be out here. He keeps escaping the nursing home, coming here to the park and telling people he's John D. Rockefeller. He even somehow got checks printed up with that name on it, can you believe it?"

The old man gave him a friendly wave as she led him away.

The stunned businessman stood there frozen in place. For the past year, he had been wheeling and dealing based on the belief that if he failed, he had that check in his safe to fall back on. But the check was a fake the whole time.

And then the businessman smiled. He realized the check had been worth a lot more than $500,000 – because it bought him back his self-confidence. Which was all he really needed in the first place.

This story was told to me by a friend, the famous business expert Brian Tracy – and I'm using it in this chapter to illustrate a very important point: What you believe is what dictates your success. Self-confidence isn't about being arrogant or egotistical – it's about believing in yourself and your ability to perform in the face of difficult outside circumstances.

That old saying, "I'll believe it when I see it," has it all wrong. The real truth is you see it when you believe it. In other words, when you believe you can accomplish something, that's when you'll actually see that accomplishment come to fruition.

Now - let's build on this idea with a few lessons from the wizard.

The wizard I'm talking about is *The Wizard of Oz*. I'm assuming you've seen the 1939 film version starring Judy Garland – most people I know, including me, viewed it on television as a child. But, believe it or not, there are a lot of ideas in there that are important for adults to take on board as well.

Start with the very last scene, where Dorothy wakes up back at home and – Spoiler Alert! - realizes her entire trip to Oz was just a dream that happened after she was knocked unconscious by the tornado. Anyway, the girl is lying in bed and says, "…if I ever go looking for my heart's desire again, I won't look any further than my own backyard; because if it isn't there, I never really lost it to begin with."

To me, that's the meaning of the movie - and it has relevance for all of us.

I think too many times, people go looking outside for solutions to their problems, challenges, and difficulties. They think they need some elusive thing that will somehow magically make them better. Sometimes they even try to be other people! Yes, it's great to emulate the qualities of people that have achieved great things, people that you admire – but you should never try to actually *be* that person. You inevitably become a pale imitation – because *that's not who you are.*

Instead, you should become the best possible version of you.

While it's great to get knowledge, support and help from outside people and institutions, your most profound answers actually come from within. The businessman in the story I just related didn't really need that $500,000 check to save him – he just needed to get his bearings, dig in and do what he needed to do. Likewise, you really don't have to go anywhere else to tap into your own potential – that potential is already within you. Other gurus and experts don't have all your answers. And I certainly don't. *You* have all those answers. Other people can only help you find them.

Think about the other characters in *The Wizard of Oz* who have undertaken quests. The Tin Man is looking for a heart. The Cowardly Lion? He just needs some courage. And the Scarecrow, of course, believes he needs a brain. They're looking to get all these things from the Wizard – and they do.

Except they don't.

Like our businessman, the Tin Man, the Lion and the Scarecrow *already* had everything they needed. The Tin Man had the heart to care for Dorothy's plight, the Scarecrow had the brains to help get them through their difficult journey, and, when push came to shove, the Lion showed the courage he thought he lacked.

What the Wizard did for this trio was make them *believe* they had the things they thought they were missing – by giving them things that were as phony as the check from "John D. Rockefeller." The Tin Man received a clock masquerading as a heart, the Scarecrow received a college degree and the Lion received an award. These were all external things that supplied them with the self-confidence to access the qualities they already had. But all the Wizard really gave them was... self-confidence.

Self-confidence. So much springs from that.

So ask yourself – is there anything external that you believe you need and are overly fixated on? Do you believe you require something outside yourself - money, status, a better car, a nicer wardrobe, the right romantic partner – to really become the person you want to be?

Then maybe you should think again. Maybe you should think about what steps you can take right this minute to start realizing your potential – *without* having those other things. Because the reality is you don't have them at this moment – and you might not *ever* have them if you don't believe in yourself and all that you can do on your own.

The head of Starbucks, Howard Schultz, grew up in a housing project constructed for the poor. Oprah Winfrey is from an impoverished family in Mississippi. Ralph Lauren started as a salesclerk at Brooks Brothers, wondering if maybe men's ties could be a little better designed. I'm sure you can come up with your own examples of people who literally started with nothing and worked their way up to becoming huge successes – because there are an awful lot of them.

I'm closing this section of the book, which focuses on performance and productivity, with this chapter on self-confidence because it really is the foundation of success. It empowers you to take risks and be proactive in the world. That in turn, enables you to accomplish things – which gives you even *more* self-confidence.

You don't have to go off to see the Wizard. Just believe in who you are and what you can do.

Then…go do it!

SUPER SCORECARD #12

Superpower:	**Self-Confidence**
Allows you to:	**Realize Your Own Potential**
Obtained by:	**Believing in Yourself**
Arch Enemy:	**Insecurity and Negativity**

PART 3
YOUR ARCH-VILLAINS:
DEFEATING THE ENEMIES
OF SUCCESS

"Man has no greater enemy than himself."
— PETRARCH

I don't know if you remember a movie from a few years ago entitled *Unbreakable* – but it was probably the weirdest cinematic superhero saga ever made. It was so weird that the main guy, Bruce Willis, spent most of the movie moping around – not even realizing he was a superhero until the very end!

And what does his self-discovery result in? Samuel L. Jackson, who makes his acquaintance in the film, comes to the conclusion that he is, in fact, Willis' archenemy! He says to Willis at the end of the film, *"It all makes sense! In a comic, you know how you can tell who the arch-villain's going to be? He's the exact opposite of the hero. And most times they're friends, like you and me!"*

He's right, folks. Lex Luthor was Superman's friend as a teenager and it was the same deal with the Green Goblin and Spiderman. It's definitely a thing. And it's my slightly long-winded way of informing you that the greatest enemies of your success may, in fact, be posing as your friends *right this second.*

Take, for example, whoever's in your head telling you that important project can wait - so why not watch some dumb TV instead? Well, anybody who lets you off the hook like that sure feels like a pal, right?

Or how about that other friendly voice in your brain – the one saying a couple of donuts won't really hurt your new diet? You gotta love anything that steers you towards extra deliciousness, of course.

Or do you?

In both of the above examples, you're dealing with antagonists tempting you away from your real, true long-term goals – and only offering short-term relief or pleasure in their place. And that's what makes our arch-villains such worthy adversaries. They can make us feel incredibly wonderful for a few moments – while causing us to sabotage the efforts that bring a lifetime of happiness.

In this next section of the book, I'm going to identify a few of these oh-too-common rascals and rogues that are hard to get out of your head – and show you how to elevate your individual powers so you can successfully defeat them, time and time again.

So – put on that cape again. We've got a few more battles to win, Super-You!

ARCH-VILLAIN #1: THE NONDECIDER

The Nondecider. This villain will literally have you running around in circles, chasing your own tail, until you're too tired and confused to get anything accomplished.

What are the warning signs that the Nondecider is about to strike?

You wake up and suddenly feel unsure of the best way to brush your teeth. Side-to-side or up-and-down? Then there's breakfast. Cereal? Some fruit? Both together?

Your head's already pounding. You go on with an empty stomach and dirty teeth, thinking all this will pass.

Then you remember with a shudder and a gasp – you have to get dressed!

After an hour of staring into your closet, you collapse to the floor in a sobbing heap, and then crawl back to your bed.

The Nondecider has won another round!

Now, the above may sound silly, but I assure you, almost every one of us has days where we just don't want the responsibility of having to make any choices. Sometimes it just feels like too much pressure. Most of us have significant others with needs, children who rely on us for guidance, an occupation with ongoing accountability, and all the other random day-to-day difficulties that we search for ways to surmount.

Face it, people, it's a lot – and that's exactly when we're the most vulnerable to the destructive powers of the Nondecider.

The Nondecider is the guy who tells us we can decide - by not deciding! Can't figure out what to get your spouse for their birthday?

Conveniently "forget!" Not sure which car to buy? Play "Paper, Rock, Scissors!" with the guy in the cubicle next to you. Don't know who the best candidate in an election is? Choose whoever's name is higher in the alphabet! That's the kind of thing that can happen when the Nondecider launches an attack.

And how does he attack? Well, first of all, the Nondecider has the power to smite you with what I call "analysis paralysis" – the inability to choose an option because you can't stop researching and reviewing information relevant to your decision. These days, that process can take you a few centuries. Here's how bad the information overload is in the 21st Century: According to one study I read, there's been more data generated in the past three years that in the previous 40,000 years of human history *combined* (as anyone who's active on Facebook already undoubtedly knows). And that is why the Nondecider stands tall, cackling loudly throughout the land as all of us tremble, dreading the next internet posting.

So – how do we take down this guy?

How do you make quick, yet thoughtful, decisions? Decisions that are, hopefully, more often right than wrong? After all, defeating the Nondecider is critical to your future. If you want to be recognized for your leadership, either at home or on the job, you need to make prompt, firm decisions. As a matter of fact, it's a defining characteristic of all great leaders. Decisiveness builds confidence in your team as well as trust in you.

Fear not – for the knowledge I'm about to share will neutralize the Nondecider every time.

First of all, as we've already discussed earlier in this book, you need to have a plan in place – with realistic, attainable objectives built in. When you've created that plan and devised those goals (and, just as importantly, completely believe in them), then it's much, much easier to make a decision, even if when it seems like a tough call.

Just approach your choice from this vantage point: Which option more closely aligns with your plan, as well as advances you towards your next goal? That's the advantage of having your plans and goals front and center in your thinking at all times – you need only compare your alternatives in terms of those plans and goals. When you're able to do that, the Nondecider will be begging for mercy before you know it.

However, he still has one more very potent weapon at his disposal – and that's your fear of making a mistake. You could be thinking that if you make a decision too quickly, too easily – well, then, maybe it's the wrong one. Don't you have to sweat these things out?

Well, no, you don't, if you have confidence in your choices. To be honest, we're all human, we all make mistakes. We can never have all the facts at our disposal nor can we ever know what's going to happen tomorrow – most of our decisions come down to making our "best guess." But being decisive is all about moving forward in the face of uncertainty, having the courage to take advantage of opportunities before they slip away, and leading not only yourself but those around you to the achievement of desirable goals.

No question about it, when you make a decision, you're putting your own judgment on the line for everyone to see. But just having the willingness to *make* that decision automatically ups the amount of respect you receive from others. So, yes, bravery makes a big difference. Just imagine a competition between two teams. The first is a team of mice, led by a lion. The second? A team of lions led by a mouse. I'll take the team led by the lion anytime.

Provided he doesn't eat the mice first, of course.

Here's what I've found over the years. As you build your decision-making muscles, as you repeatedly rebuff the Nondecider's attacks, you'll find that the quality of your decisions improves as much as the quantity. Don't get me wrong, I'm not advocating you go off half-cocked making snap judgments without having any of the facts – but what I am saying is there is a point where too much information and too much hemming and hawing becomes destructive to your agenda. The more decisions you make, the more you'll understand where exactly that point is – and the better the choices you'll make will become.

Be brave. Be decisive. But be smart.

Oh, and hold your toothbrush at a 45-degree angle to your gums, and make an up-and-down motion.

You're welcome.

(By the way, in this section of the book? We're going to give you a few handy Arch-Villain Scorecards instead of Super Scorecards, so you can keep track of these bothersome bad guys!)

ARCH-VILLAIN SCORECARD #1

Supervillain:	**The Nondecider**
Wants You to:	**Avoid Making Choices**
Wins When:	**You Fail to Act**
Defeated by:	**Decisiveness and Confidence**

ARCH-VILLAIN #2: MR. TUNNELVISION

The fact is, you never see Mr. Tunnelvision coming.

As a matter of fact, thanks to him, you don't see a *lot* of things coming.

Mr. Tunnelvision's unique way of creating mischief ensures that you never see the big picture – just a very small square of it. For example, maybe you obsess about a luxury vacation you want to take but can't afford – and, as a result, ignore the work that could increase your income enough to take that luxury vacation. Or, perhaps you have a very specific vision of what the perfect mate for you *must* look like – which causes you to unwittingly let your soulmate walk out of your life because that person has the wrong hair color.

As you can see, Mr. Tunnelvision can do a ton of damage. And what's really dangerous about this foe is he has science on his side.

Your brain, my brain, everyone's brain has a special feature called the Reticular Activating System (RAS). Now, don't get me wrong, RAS is an organic mechanism you definitely need to have working for you; otherwise, you might not be able to make sense of anything. That's because the RAS takes all the tremendous amount of information and stimuli that the world throws your way on a daily basis and sorts it out for you, so that you can understand how things fit together. Basically, it figures out what's important to you and then directs you to pay attention to it.

For example, let's say you just learned a new word you never heard before. Just after you learn it, it suddenly seems like everyone around you is using the exact same word. What a coincidence!

Well, not really. You probably heard the word before, but didn't notice it. Now, because you're newly aware of it, it rings a little alarm bell in your mind every time it pops out of someone's mouth.

The same phenomenon can take place when you buy a new car. All at once, you constantly notice that make and model on the streets more than any other kind of car – as if everyone suddenly ran out and bought the same vehicle that you did (RAS can make you feel like a real trendsetter). However, the truth is you're newly aware of that particular car and hyper-attentive to its appearance.

Basically, your RAS helps you discover needles in haystacks. It helps you sort out the tons of information we spoke about in the last chapter and find what's relevant to you and your life. Here's an example of how it frequently it helps you out: If you're walking through a crowded and noisy airport, and your name is announced over the Public Address system, your RAS causes you to zero in on that in a flash - even while the content of other announcements flies by without you bothering to take any of it in.

So how can your RAS be a bad thing? How can it actually aid and abet the master scoundrel known as Mr. Tunnelvision?

Simple. Just as you can be focused on a new word or your new car, you can also be focused on what's wrong with your life – which, in turn, causes you to amplify whatever negative thing you encounter and completely ignore all the positives.

And that's when Mr. Tunnelvision rubs his hands with glee. Because he's got you right where he wants you – down in the dumps, neglecting every opportunity for success, and covered in ANTs.

Well, let me tell you something. You've got to STOMP those ANTs.

Now, before you report me to PETA (although I'm not sure what their position on the insect world happens to be), let me be clear that I'm not talking about our six-legged friends with whom we share many a picnic. No, the ANT I'm talking about is a three-letter acronym for "Always and Never Thinking." When we engage in ANTs, we leave ourselves wide open to Mr. Tunnelvision's nefarious schemes, because ANTs disempower us and turn us into victims.

When you're employing Always and Never Thinking, you tend to make statements like:

- I *always* get stuck in traffic.
- I *never* have my ideas chosen.
- I *always* get ignored at work.
- I can *never* get ahead in life.

When you cement those opinions into place as fact, guess what? Your RAS causes you to notice the times those bad things happen – and ignore the times when they don't. That further validates your Always and Never Thinking – and further weakens your ability to both see and build on good things that happen to you.

People who engage in ANTs assume they're just being brutally honest about their lot in life – but the real truth is "Always" and "Never" statements, are, at their core, dishonest. Nothing, of course, is an absolute in life. More importantly, negative situations can be transformed into positive ones.

Let's take a simple example – the statement, "I always get stuck in traffic." Well, if you are frequently staring at the back of a non-moving bumper, perhaps you should ask what you can do to alleviate the situation. You could, for example, try another route. Or maybe change your working hours to avoid rush hour. If you can't change those hours, perhaps you could leave earlier to beat the traffic - and bring along something fun or productive to do before you have to actually begin working. Or, if all else fails, maybe you can start listening to audio books or podcasts while you're stuck in the car to make the long trip more enjoyable or educational.

Now, let's get a little more complex and tackle the statement, "I never can get ahead in life." Forgetting for a moment that you must have gotten ahead at one point or another – otherwise, you'd still be in diapers in your crib – think about *why* you feel frustrated about where you are. Is it time to change jobs? Even your career? Are you making an effort to get "unstuck?" Are you honestly evaluating your skills, talents and mindsets so you can make the most of what you have?

My challenge to you is, whenever you find yourself in an ANT state of mind, whenever you say to yourself it's always this or never that, recognize that you're automatically putting yourself in a psychological box. Recognize it and, more importantly, try to disprove what you're saying. I guarantee it won't be hard. Either it's not true and you're playing the victim – or you're in some kind of negative pattern that you can break free of.

It's up to you – for the only way to keep Mr. Tunnelvision out of your business is to look at life with a wider lens.

ARCH-VILLAIN SCORECARD #2

Supervillain:	**Mr. Tunnelvision**
Wants You to:	**Lose Sight of Opportunities**
Wins When:	**You Only See a Small Part of the Picture**
Defeated by:	**Expand Your Thinking**

ARCH-VILLAIN #3: THE PERFORMANCE BUSTER

Good sucks.

Shocked that I, Ed DeCosta, believer in all good things, would say those two little words?

Well, I have a good reason.

Feeling good about everything leads to complacency. Why rock the boat if everything's good? Why bother trying?

That's why, when you feel good about your life, your work, about everything...the Performance Buster feels friggin' GREAT. Because he knows he's won another victory over the forces of excellence.

You see, the Performance Buster's real villainy isn't about preventing you from doing something. No, he wants to prevent you from doing something *exceptionally well*. Because if you make an extra effort to do your best, you'll be recognized and even rewarded for it – and he really, really hates that.

And that's why good sucks. Because people think good...is good enough.

Complacency kills. It kills initiative and drive. It drains the energy we need to create change in our lives. We end up settling for where we are and I think that is the biggest shame in the world. Why? Because, eventually, your potential, your ability to do more, be more, give more and, yes, have more is going to be completely untapped. Eventually, all that potential withers and dies due to atrophy. And if you don't know what atrophy means, it's this, according to the dictionary: "a gradual decline in effectiveness or vigor due to underuse or neglect." To put it in more basic terms, if you don't use it, you lose it.

So let go of the good and let some pain in your life. Because, to soar, you must get sore.

The other day, I got out of the shower in the morning and thought to myself, "Boy, are my legs hurting." Why the pain? Because of a work-out I had the day before. I had a trainer who pushed me beyond the usual because he knew I have certain physical goals I want to reach. To move towards those goals, I had to do some hard work – and that hard work resulted in some pain.

But, as they say, no pain, no gain. There are no shortcuts. You have to do the hard work and that's going to give you some hurt.

By the way, I'm talking about more than physical exercise.

As I've noted, I talk to business owners and leaders quite often – and a lot of the talk is about what's preventing them from reaching their objectives. And many times, it's because they're avoiding…pain. Not physical pain, but emotional pain.

For instance, one of my clients had an ongoing problem with a trusted associate, someone who rose through the ranks as the organization was just beginning to grow. Unfortunately, it's a fact of life that sometimes the people who are invaluable during your company's initial growth end up lacking the skill-set to continue that role when the business becomes much bigger. My client had to face a hard truth – this person was actually getting in the company's way and needed to be moved to another, lesser role.

Of course, this was a very emotional decision for this client. It would involve some psychic pain, because he was friends with this person. But when someone is holding you or your business back, something has to be done. It's not fair to the staffer to pretend he or she is doing the job that needs to be done – and it's not fair to everyone else in the company to lose out on continued growth.

Sometimes progress hurts. Most of the time it hurts.

But to soar, you must get sore.

Here's another strategy for taking on the Performance Buster – and it involves three little words: Think, Feel and Do. It also involves a little more brain science, the kind we delved into in the last chapter.

Most of you have heard of cognitive intelligence (measured by IQ, our intelligence quotient) and affective intelligence (measured by our EQ, our emotional intelligence). Both your intellectual and your emotional abilities are essential, of course, to fully engaging with ambitious goals.

But there's actually a *third* leg to this particular stool.

It's called conation and it pertains to our ability to take action. We can think about doing something - and we can feel like doing something - but if we don't actually *do* that something, what's the point? Conation provides the answer – because it supplies the impulse to take action.

So – what sparks our conation? What makes us buck the Performance Buster and be proactive? Well, the research I've reviewed connects it all back to a one-word question: "Why?" In other words, what prompts you to take action is when you understand *why* something needs to be done – why it's necessary or in your best interests to do so. That's what fuels motivation, inspiration, persistence - all the qualities that help you perform to the best of your abilities.

So if you want to perform at a higher level, click into the conation area of your brain. Don't just focus on what has to be done – focus on *why* it has to be done. To be more specific, think of the goal you'll achieve or the benefit you'll gain by doing the task in question. Use the same process for when you want to inspire others around you to be more effective. Help them understand what they're going to get out of their actions. That in turn will motivate them to overcome obstacles and give their best to get the job done.

Uncover the "Why" – and watch the Performance Buster wonder why he's so helpless against you.

I'd like to end this particular chapter by talking about a man who really has the Performance Buster's number. You've probably heard the old saying, "I cried because I had no shoes until I met a man that had no feet." There are many lessons that you can take from that proverb, but the main one is not to get obsessed with your own particular challenges – because there's someone out there who has far greater challenges in front of them.

I don't know that the true meaning of that saying has ever reverberated with me more than when I met Nick Vujicic, a motivational speaker from Australia.

If you don't know the name, Nick is a man who was born with no arms and no legs – but still manages to be a lot more influential and powerful than many people who have all their limbs. His YouTube videos alone have millions of viewers.

Getting to meet Nick and hear him speak was a profound experience. I suggest you look him up on the internet yourself to get his full message – but I'd like to share a few of the key takeaways I received from hearing him speak.

1. You don't know what your limits are until you've reached them. As you know, many people talk about this idea, but hearing it from Nick gave it a whole new depth of meaning. You literally don't know what you're capable of until you've tried – and that means, yes, you're going to fail a few times, but that's part of the process.

2. Failure isn't really the right word for when you do try and don't succeed. The proper term is "education." You gain a great big learning experience that enables you, when you go back to the drawing board and try again, to understand what mistakes you made and how to avoid them. Don't make failing a big negative; instead, focus on how you can do things better next time.

3. Obstacles are truly opportunities – so look at whatever is standing in your way as something to take advantage of. This is a very different way of looking at life and it will take a lot of determination

and practice to achieve this kind of mindset. But the effort is worth it. Let your obstacles and challenges energize you instead of defeating you.

In conclusion, keep moving forward as fast as you can and as hard as you can. The Performance Buster isn't difficult to outrun. As a matter of fact, he only overtakes you when you're content to stay at a standstill.

ARCH-VILLAIN SCORECARD #3

Supervillain:	The Performance Buster
Wants You to:	Settle for Less from Yourself
Wins When:	You Say, "That's Good Enough"
Defeated by:	Doing What It Takes to Reach Full Potential

ARCH-VILLAIN #4: THE MESSAGE BLOCKER

Got something to say?

That's all well and good with the do-badder known as the Message Blocker. He doesn't care if you attempt to communicate with other people. He's just out to make sure that whoever's on the receiving end completely misunderstands what you're saying.

As the late great George Bernard Shaw once said, "The single biggest problem with communication is the illusion that it has taken place." Whether you're talking face-to-face, posting on social media or texting on your smartphone, all too often what you say doesn't convey what you mean – for a variety of reasons. Age, culture, nationality, language and misunderstood humor can all come into play when you find your words are completely misinterpreted. How many times have you read about someone who has blown his or her career because of a dumb joke posted on Twitter?

As you can see, the Message Blocker has a lot of tools at his disposal.

Even when you go out of your way to be clear, you still can run afoul of this fiend. For example, many of us happen to believe in the power of the written word. What could be clearer than a statement in an email? After all, it's right there in black and white, correct? So there can't possibly be any room for a questionable interpretation.

Cue the game show buzzer that loudly indicates "WRONG." And here's the proof.

I want to share with you my favorite eight-word sentence: "I never said you stole my red bicycle." Does that seem like a simple and clear-cut statement?

Far from it. I mean halfway around the world far from it. I mean *light years* away from it.

If it's so clear-cut, choose from the following options:

- Is this sentence about who stole your red bicycle? ("I never said YOU stole my red bicycle.")
- Is it about what color bicycle got stolen? ("I never said you stole my RED bicycle.")
- Is it about what item actually got stolen? ("I never said you stole my red BICYCLE.")
- Or is it about determining whether the bicycle was borrowed - or just plain taken? ("I never said you STOLE my red bicycle.")

The truth is, this made-up sentence of mine *can have any one of the above four meanings* – but only *one* of those meanings was intended. And that's the kind of ambiguity the Message Blocker derives his power from.

Here's how to block the Message Blocker from creating havoc with your communications.

First of all, confirm your understanding when you receive an important message or if someone tells you something you really need to know. You don't have to repeat every word, but simply say, "What I hear you saying is..." and then quickly summarize the content as you perceive it, especially if there's a lot in it. For instance, if it's a business conversation, then repeat back the particulars - the data, the dates, the deliverables, etc. When the other person confirms you got it right, then you can relax.

This is a system that's always in place when communication is absolutely critical. For example, have you ever heard a pilot speak to a control tower? I had that opportunity when I rode in a private plane as a copilot and was able to listen in. Both sides confirmed what the other party just said, by saying something like, "Roger that. Proceeding 19,000 feet on a heading of..." And so on (I actually don't speak pilot, so that's as far as I can demonstrate, but you get the idea.). Lives are literally at stake in these cases - so all concerned take the time to make sure everyone's clear on what's going on.

Second of all, don't accept gossip as gospel. There's a familiar game most of you played as a kid called, variously, "Whispers Down the Alley," "Broken Telephone," "Pass the Whispers," etc. The concept is terrifyingly simple – you line up a bunch of people in a row. The first person in the row whispers a sentence to the next person, that person whispers what he or she hears to the next person, and so on and so on, until the message finally reaches the last person in line.

99.9% of the time, the sentence has been mangled beyond belief by the time it gets to the last person – often to the point where no words of the original remain in the final version. You might start with, "The yellow car won the race" – and end up with "Throw spaghetti in your face."

Gossip creates the same kind of confusion. It especially tends to emphasize the negative aspects of whatever rumor's being spread. Someone who might have simply had a difficult day at an office could in a few hours be perceived as a worker who's on the verge of being fired!

Finally, here's one last quick tip on how to handcuff the Message Blocker.

Most people stink at delivering bad news. Who likes to upset another person? The danger, however, comes from when you sugarcoat bad news to such an extent that the person doesn't actually *hear* the bad news – because you never really come out and say what you have to.

It's more important to be as straight-forward with bad news than with any other kind of news. People have to understand the situation as clearly as possible, and they can't do that if you're beating around the bush.

I work hard at that clarity – and that resulted in one of the oddest compliments I've ever gotten in my life. After a long planning session for a big meeting a client was preparing for, this client said to me, "Ed – you're mean…in a nice way."

Well, that confused me – so I asked him to elaborate.

His answer? "You tell me the truth, you speak bluntly, you speak frankly, but you're kind about it." Once I understood what he was saying, I was pleased he felt that way. I believe the best way to make a hard truth go down the easiest is to do it in a kind-hearted and constructive manner. But it's still a hard truth, so people usually aren't interested in admiring my technique in delivering it!

So lay out the facts when you have to deliver some harsh reality. The Message Blocker won't thank you…but the recipient of the bad news just might.

ARCH-VILLAIN SCORECARD #4

Supervillain:	**The Message Blocker**
Wants You to:	**Miscommunicate**
Wins When:	**You Allow Ambiguity**
Defeated by:	**Straight Talk with Confirmation**

ARCH-VILLAIN #5: THE DISTRACTION DRIVER

"**H**ey, about those Red Sox?"

That's something the Distraction Driver is always whispering in my ear during baseball season. He wants me to forget what I should be thinking about – and he's frequently successful. He's a smart guy, that Distraction Driver – because no matter what's going on with my favorite team, I'm going to want to talk about it. If they're doing well, I want to go on about how great they are. If they're not…well, sorry, but I want you to share in my misery.

Has there ever been a bigger boom time for the Distraction Driver? I don't think so. Go watch diners at a restaurant. Are they talking to each other? Some are, but most are checking their smartphones for the latest tweet or Facebook update. That's just what makes the Distraction Driver such a worthy foe: He's able to disrupt your most important thought processes with something inconsequential that really doesn't matter.

Although, of course, the Red Sox *do matter*. But anyway…

Here's how much damage the explosion of mobile gadgets has done to our brains. Driver. According to an NBC report, in 2000, the average attention span was 12 seconds. In 2013? It was down to 8 seconds. That's, of course, a staggering $1/3^{rd}$ drop in 13 years.

But why am I even bothering to relay this information? You stopped reading this after the first two paragraphs to play Candy Crush on your phone!

But, for the four or five of you who made it this far, let me explain why it's important to resist the Distraction Driver whenever possible.

Most transformational efforts in your life require long-term focus. Rome wasn't built in a day – and neither was any other achievement that has any lasting power. Therefore, any person who wants to reach their highest goals must possess the power to concentrate on those objectives on a daily basis.

When you train yourself to do that, the Distraction Driver doesn't stand a chance.

With that in mind, here's my NUMBER ONE secret to defeating this disruptive dude. It's a pretty simple piece of advice – and you've probably heard it before – but maybe you need to hear it again. Here it is:

Do one thing at a time.

Don't multitask. When you do, some aspect of your work suffers. Indeed, even some aspect of your life can suffer, such as when you try to spend quality time with a family member and end up on your phone for hours on a business call.

So plan your work – use a calendar. Don't constantly check email and social media sites – that's just other people's priorities interfering in your life. Map out a strategy and a schedule that recognizes your highest priorities and allows you to give them your full attention.

Can you defeat the Distraction Driver with such a pathetic little weapon as a simple kitchen timer? Yes, you can – I use one myself. It's an accountability partner that only costs you a few dollars but can help make you a whole lot more – because they help you deliver your highest level of work. Simply decide how long you're going to work on something, set the timer for the amount of minutes you've designated for that day – and don't let anything other than maybe the apocalypse get in your way.

And remember, I said, "maybe."

The biggest myth about productivity is that you're super-efficient if you're getting ten things done at once. When you're trying to write a proposal while checking your email while talking to a client while you're feeding the dog, all at the same time - well, you're just asking for the Distraction Driver to swoop in and cause you to be so careless, you end up putting your proposal in your pooch's dog dish.

It's rare that you can combine quantity with quality – and so much better when you don't even try.

Also, look for things that help you focus. For instance, I feel as though I read with much more concentration and comprehension when I play classical music in the background. The music provides a gentle bed that shields me from other thoughts that might sneak into my head. On the other hand, when I'm trying to accomplish an intensive task and I have ESPN blaring in the background – well, that's just not happening.

My final tip involves a tip of the hat to the inspirational author and speaker Stephen Covey, who wrote the best-seller, *The Seven Habits of Highly Effective People*. The seventh habit he cites in that book? "Sharpen the Saw." If you don't know what that's all about, let me just say it has nothing to do with tools – and everything to do with keeping yourself in prime condition.

You see, the Distraction Driver is never more powerful than when you're worn out. When you're burning the candle at both ends, you're constantly looking for quick and easy escapes – and DD is happy to provide them. All studies show that the more tired you are, the more susceptible you are to being distracted and, frankly, making crucial mistakes. You just don't have the stamina to stay properly focused on anything.

Sharpening the Saw simply means you're taking the time to refresh yourself, mentally, emotionally, spiritually and physically – so burnout doesn't happen. When I coach people in an effort to improve their performance, believe it or not, we do spend time talking about downtime – and because you should take the time to reward yourself for the hard work you do. It's a crucial part of sustaining your performance in your work.

So get proper rest. Take a break or even a vacation when you feel you need it. Spend time with people you enjoy being around and who you love. Recently, my family and I had an amazing week in South Beach in Miami, Florida. The only thing we had to worry about was whether it was going to be sunny or not – which we had no control over. Whatever choices we did have to make – well, none of the options were bad ones.

It was a carefree week, the kind you rarely get to have as an adult – which is why carving out space for that kind of vacation is important. You can even pull it off in a weekend - I also recently went on a white water rafting adventure with my sons and, even though it lasted less than 48 hours, I came home feeling energized and refreshed.

And that, in turn, caused the Distraction Driver to engage in behavior he usually tries to make others do: He looked elsewhere.

ARCH-VILLAIN SCORECARD #5

Supervillain:	**The Distraction Driver**
Wants You to:	**Take Your Eye Off the Ball**
Wins When:	**Lose Sight of Priorities**
Defeated by:	**Planning and Focus**

ARCH-VILLAIN #6: THE PROCRASTINATOR

You don't have to prepare for when the Procrastinator shows up to do battle.

That's because if you wait for the Procrastinator....well, that's all you're going to do. Wait...and wait...and wait. And wait some more. As you may have guessed, he takes his time showing up.

Actually, what he's really doing is taking *your* time.

The Procrastinator has this in common with the Distraction Driver from our last chapter – they both gobble up time as though it was candy. But, while the Distraction Driver keeps your eye *off* the ball, the Procrastinator never even lets you get to it. He simply causes you to put off tasks until the very last minute – which ensures that you'll try to do them too quickly and, as a result, not very well.

His master stroke? Making you *complain* that you don't have enough time to get things done – when in reality you had all the time in the world!

The Procrastinator tells you to go ahead and put things off. You don't have to worry about all those nagging problems you need to solve right this minute. That report for work? It's not due for two weeks. Your taxes? They don't have to be filed for a month. That aching tooth? You can stand the pain for a while, why go to the dentist and let yourself in for more pain?

And then, of course, a simple cavity filling turns into an expensive and very uncomfortable root canal.

The Procrastinator knows it's easy to let things go until it's too late – especially if those things are unpleasant to deal with in the first place. "Let tomorrow take care of itself" is his motto. It's a lot more fun to binge watch shows on Netflix, check out what people are doing on Facebook, or just go get some ice cream.

By the way, in case you didn't know, the Procrastinator knows you love ice cream.

So - how do you battle this foul fiend? How do you deflect delaying everything on your to-do list? You might think time management would do the trick. But actually, believe it or not, I think time management is a myth. Maybe this is just a matter of semantics on my part, but, to me, time is the one commodity you *can't* manage – because everybody, from the richest zillionaire to the lowliest poverty-stricken poor soul on earth gets exactly the same amount of time: 168 hours a week. That's 24 hours multiplied by 7 days, of course, and that's all we get – and, of course, we lose about a third of that time to sleep, leaving us roughly 112 hours left to get things done.

Is that enough time to take care of everything? Don't waste your breath asking that question – because it HAS to be enough. We have no choice. We can't "manage" to manufacture more time than we already have.

And that's why we must put off the Procrastinator whenever he tries to eat up any part of those 112 hours. It's the only way to become truly productive.

The best defense against the Procrastinator is a simple one: Scheduling. When you work out a schedule, you're able to put "first things first" and remind yourself of your priorities. You put your top priorities first in your calendar so they become immovable objects – the "Big Rocks of Life," as Dr. Stephen Covey once called them. This is the single most effective way you can increase your productivity that I've experienced – you simply stop the little pebbles in your life from getting in the way of those big rocks. It's also how you avoid delaying doing what needs to get done and how you stop helping the Procrastinator feel as though he's won (what's left of) the day.

For me, the scheduling process begins on Sunday evening. That's when I plan all those hours of the week to the best of my abilities (and I will freely admit another time or day might work better for you - it truly doesn't matter as long as you do it on a weekly basis). I begin by identifying my priorities for the week. Is a work project pressing that requires most of my time? Do I need to get back on top of my exercise regimen? Are there some contacts I need to make sure to touch bases with – even get together with? Do I need to check the books to see that my financials are in order?

It all should come down to answering a big two-part question: Where am I, now, at the beginning of the week – and where do I want to be (even, in some cases, *need* to be) at the end of the week?

If you want to give this level of scheduling a try, I heartily encourage you to do so. But know one thing in advance, before you schedule one single block of time - you are not going to clear out all the current unfinished business in your life in the next 7 days.

I tell you this to help you avoid a big pitfall: When you first begin scheduling your weeks, there is a temptation to overschedule and try to accomplish too much at once. That just leaves you too exhausted to even think about scheduling the next week. It's more important to look at this as an ongoing activity and pace yourself. It will take a few weeks to find your groove through trial and error, but, if you stick to it, you'll settle into a scheduling mindset where you intuitively understand what's realistic and what isn't.

Nevertheless, do try as hard as you might, particularly in the first weeks of your scheduling, to stick to what you put down on paper. Otherwise – the Procrastinator will be making sure you put off until tomorrow what should be done today.

Of course, scheduling isn't enough to stop the Procrastinator from disrupting your life. Writing out what you're going to do isn't really helpful – unless you actually follow through and do the things you plan to do. You need one other arrow in your quiver to shoot at this arch-enemy – and that's *initiative*.

"Initiative" comes from the Latin word meaning "beginning." Which is appropriate, since, to me, the key to getting things done is to actually get started on them. Quite often, I encounter people who talk about the things they're going to do, but then never even take a stab at getting them done. It's like a runner who doesn't even show up at the starting line – he or she certainly isn't going to complete that race. On the other hand, a runner that starts is, barring an injury, definitely going to finish. That first step can be the most important one, especially if it creates the momentum that carries you through to the end.

That first step, however, can also be the most difficult one.

As they say, sometimes it can feel like your get-up-and-go got up and went – and your initiative is at a low ebb. Maybe you didn't sleep well the night before. Maybe an unexpected crisis threw your day out of whack. Whatever the reason, you're not in the mood to make a move.

That's when your initiative can use a helper.

I've touched on the notion of an accountability partner earlier in this book – someone you know and trust who holds your feet to the fire and makes sure you follow through on what you say you're going to do. I want to reemphasize the importance of that person here – particularly when you're implementing this kind of scheduling process. Your accountability partner doesn't have to be your boss or your significant other - it can be anyone.

The best results, however, come from people who understand you and understand what you do. And it doesn't have to be a one-way street. I often recommend that two people with similar backgrounds, occupations or high demands on their time form an accountability partnership – so that each can help the other stick to their objectives and tackle their highest priorities. Both people get equal rewards out of such a relationship and both are more motivated to hold up their end as a result.

So think about starting in earnest to create a weekly schedule. Then, look for an accountability partner to keep your initiative and follow-through firing on all cylinders. Because when you do all that, the Procrastinator will most likely go seek other prey.

He's all about wasting other people's time – not his own.

ARCH-VILLAIN SCORECARD #6

Supervillain:	The Procrastinator
Wants You to:	Never Get to Important Tasks
Wins When:	You Delay What You Need to Do
Defeated by:	Scheduling, Initiative and Accountability

ARCH-VILLAIN #7: THE NOWHERE MAN

"The most repulsive group of men I've ever seen," declared the late TV host and pundit, David Susskind.

The year was 1965 and he was talking about the Beatles.

Today, the Beatles are, of course, regarded as a legendary rock band that changed the face of music forever. Back in the day, however, many regarded them as a scourge on humanity and a threat to America's well-being.

The backlash to the Beatles in the early 60's was so severe that other musical acts released a series of record singles designed to bring the Fab Four down. Songs like "The Beatles Just Got to Go," "Beatles, You Bug Me," and the most likely wrong-in-retrospect "I'm Better than the Beatles" were recorded by obscure artists who were all enraged by the English foursome's domination of the charts.

Well, luckily we can all laugh at that nonsense now – because we know the Beatles weren't really harmful to anyone. If anything, they kicked up musical standards and took modern music to places that nobody (except them) envisioned.

However.

To be completely honest, there is one thing for which I cannot forgive John, Paul, George and Ringo. One thing which I will hold against them until I take my last breath on this planet earth.

They created one of the most despicable, disreputable, disgusting arch-enemies you'll ever encounter – the Nowhere Man, which is the title of a song they recorded in 1965 (and one of the group's very first songs that had nothing to do with love or romance, by the way).

Now, I will say this in defense of the Beatles – the group merely gave this particular villain a catchy name. The reality is the Nowhere Man has undoubtedly been around as long as the human race. But the Beatles really brought him to life with this tune, giving a dead-on description with lyrics such as, "Doesn't have a point of view, knows not where he's going to, isn't he a bit like you and me?"

So what kind of threat can a Nowhere Man really pose to folks like you and me? Plenty – because his mission is to turn us all into Nowhere People. John Lennon, the Beatle who was the primary composer of the song, felt his menace directly. As Paul McCartney explains the state Lennon was in at the time he wrote the song: *"I think at that point, he was a bit...wondering where he was going, and to be truthful so was I. I was starting to worry about him."*

Paul should have been worrying. You always need to worry about anyone inclined to go Nowhere.

The Nowhere Man will cause you to drift into a state of apathy. You end up going around in circles with no goals in mind. You lack urgency in your actions and you let your life go where it will, instead of taking it in a defined direction. As the song says, "Nowhere man don't worry... take your time, don't hurry...leave it all till somebody else lends you a hand."

Why hurry? You're going nowhere. And who cares about getting somewhere?

So how do you stay out of the clutches of the Nowhere Man? How do you make sure you don't lose your mojo – and your purpose?

Well, first of all, turn up the heat.

Have you ever met somebody for the first time – and felt energy just radiating from that person? Chances are you've just encountered one of those people who I like to say is "running hot." Their minds are active and constantly connecting with those around them – and they always want to discover new and exciting things and incorporate them into their lives.

When you "run hot," you're not passively letting your days float away. No, you're actively pursuing what there is to experience. You're as far away from nowhere as you can get.

How can you turn up your own personal temperature?

I have a theory – and that is, in order to run hot, you have to *think big*. You naturally perform at a higher level when your mindset is geared towards larger goals and objectives.

Think big. Two words that pack a lot of weight.

Let's start with "think." Thinking is about taking the time to consider your highest priorities, your true purpose, spending time in what author and speaker Matthew Kelly calls, "the Classroom of Silence." You can't get caught in a nowhere cycle if you really work on developing your possibilities, your desired outcomes and identifying what you want to achieve in the coming days, weeks, months and years. This kind of thinking can be done through simple meditation or prayer if you're so inclined.

Now – let's move on to "big." We all too often limit our beliefs and put ourselves into boxes that we ourselves are responsible for constructing. We impose limitations on our lives that aren't real – and only hold us back from achieving our true potential. Remaining mediocre is another way of going nowhere – you never dare to break out of your old habits and patterns or move yourself out of your safe area to see just what you can actually accomplish. However, when you allow yourself to think big, when you look over the walls you've built around your ambitions, you raise your internal temperature and "run hot."

All because you think big.

But there's something else in play here, the powerful intangible that really controls your thermostat – and that's *belief.*

When you truly believe in yourself, you can't help but think big – because you want to be the best person you're capable of being. Some people are lucky enough to be born with that kind of confidence. Others have to develop it, but it can be done, trust me.

Which brings us to another important intangible – imagination.

By using your imagination, you visualize your own success. You can see yourself using your skills and talents to attain what you want in life. You can also imagine what it feels like to reach those precious goals and keep that special feeling inside you to motivate you in your performance. You may still be in the process of gaining the experience and the breakthroughs you'll need to have in order to succeed in the way you want to – but if you can imagine you're already where you want to be, if you can *own* your dreams, then you can move forward with the confidence to make them come true.

Turn up your heat with belief – and think big to make things happen. Then the Nowhere Man has nowhere to go but elsewhere – where he can make "all his nowhere plans for nobody."

ARCH-VILLAIN SCORECARD #7

Supervillain:	**The Nowhere Man**
Wants You to:	**Never Move Forward**
Wins When:	**You Lack Direction**
Defeated by:	**Thinking Big and Running Hot**

PART 4
DYNAMIC DUOS:
COMBOS THAT PACK A
ONE-TWO PUNCH

Macaroni & Cheese. Spaghetti & Meatballs. Milk & Cookies. They're all great together – and I'm sure you have your own favorite pair of foods that magically make each other more delicious.

The same principle applies to such famous entertainment teams as Simon & Garfunkel, Laurel & Hardy, even Bert & Ernie - twosomes who are so much more powerful together than apart.

The whole *can* be greater than the sum of its parts – and so it is with the concepts we're going to talk about in this section. Individually, they're very important – but when combined with the appropriate mate, they become super-powered. Like Batman & Robin or the Green Hornet & Kato, these dynamic duos can't be beaten – especially when it comes to providing inspiration, motivation, and, of course, ED-ification.

So get ready – I'm about to introduce you to some dominant double teams that definitely have the moves to advance your personal and professional agendas. You'll quickly see that sometimes it *does* take two – which is why it's worth putting these combos to work for you.

KNOWING AND CARING

Ever hear of someone being described sarcastically as a "Know-It-All?" Or even described someone with that name?

Most of you probably have.

It tends to happen when people use knowledge as a weapon. You could easily believe they learned everything they could just so they can feel superior to those around them. And frankly, they're not much fun to be around. They're frequently the butt of jokes in movies and TV shows, because nobody likes a Know-It-All – even other Know-It-Alls, as they don't want to be around somebody who might know as much as them!

There's obviously nothing wrong with educating yourself to the highest extent possible. As you've seen elsewhere in this book, I'm a big proponent of that. However, knowledge by itself is a cold, empty proposition. That's why one of the great leadership principles goes as follows:

People don't care about how much you know – until they know how much you care.

That's why knowing really needs to be combined with caring to be effective. If you're not displaying empathy for the people around you, they're liable to dismiss the degree of expertise you worked so hard to gain.

I recently had a conversation with someone who rejected the whole knowing and caring idea. To me, this person really overvalued how far knowledge alone was going to get him. He just wasn't interested in connecting with other people – so why would they listen to what he had to say?

People become true leaders when they successfully influence people. This trait is more important than positions, titles or other superficial markers; just because you slap a label on a person doesn't mean they possess the leadership essentials. Yes, we all want our leaders to have wisdom – but, in my opinion, the absolute best leaders are those that combine that wisdom with the ability to build caring relationships that matter. They understand that you have to touch a heart before you ask for a hand.

For example, let's talk about doctors. The ones that have the best reputations and the most people in their waiting rooms are the ones with the best bedside manner. They don't just have the necessary medical training, they also have the ability to relate to the patients and their loved ones on a human level. They avoid speaking jargon that's meaningless to the average person; instead, they word things in ways the non-medical can understand. They make the effort to genuinely *communicate*.

As a business coach, I tend to put a big emphasis on productivity and efficiency, as most coaches do. Unfortunately, that can send the wrong message to executives I coach – that it's okay if you're abrupt and coldly issue edicts to your employees in order to improve your operation. Well, it's not okay. You should get to know those that not only work with you, but also for you. If you plan to lead them, you have to connect with them.

Of course, that goes double for your family and loved ones. If you're helping your child with homework, it's not just about teaching him or her the lessons in the school book. It's also a chance to bond, show empathy and get to know that child on a deeper level (and, of course, ultimately determine if that train from Pittsburgh with 10 tons of freight going at 70 mph is going to beat that train from Cleveland with 8 tons of freight going at 90 mph to Philadelphia).

Knowing without caring is an empty pursuit. Of course, caring without knowing has its own pitfalls. We are all aware of people who have gotten promoted ahead of other, worthier co-workers simply because of their superior social skills – validating the old saw, "It's not what you know, it's who you know." That may be true in the short run, but, at some point, what you *don't* know will hang you out to dry. Ill-equipped professional climbers almost always get exposed for their lack of smarts – and suffer a hard and quick fall.

So care enough about the people around you to make genuine emotional connections – and know enough to have the needed wisdom to influence them.

DYNAMIC DUO SCORECARD #1

Dynamic Duo:	**Knowing and Caring**
Helps You:	**Become an Influential Leader**
Obtained by:	**Education and Empathy**
Makes You:	**Respected and Connected**

CHANGE AND CONSISTENCY

It's funny how a James Bond movie can make you think.

No, I'm not being sarcastic. I was recently watching one of 007's newer screen adventures, when I began to notice that there were a lot of callbacks to the older films. At the same time, however, it updated the Bond brand with some exciting new elements and 21st Century hi-tech gimmickry that hadn't been seen before. And I thought it was all done in very appealing way. If you were younger, you would probably respond to the new stuff – or, if you were older (guilty as charged), you'd enjoy the references to the original Sean Connery films. In other words, the blending of old and new created a synergy that made the movie a lot more memorable.

This doesn't only work with Her Majesty's Secret Service, by the way – we see the old and new also hook up in many industries transformed by technology. For example, I'm sitting right now in my office surrounded by shelves of hardcover books – but you can now, of course, download many of those same books and read them electronically on a reading device such as the Amazon Kindle. Then there's the music industry – which went from the vinyl albums of my youth to cassette tapes to CDs to digital files (and now, funny enough, vinyl is cool again with a lot of young people). Even when you go to a city you haven't been to in a while, like New York, you quickly notice how the new skyscrapers literally stack up against the old buildings built with the classic architecture of the 1920's and 30's.

The old informs the new – and the new refreshes the old.

That led me to thinking about how, as individuals, it's important for us to combine the old and the new as well. That's why Change and Consistency – often looked at as opposites – in reality make for a very compatible combo. But of course, to make Change and Consistency effective partners for you personally, you have to retain the best of the "old you" – and figure out what should go into the "new you."

How do you determine that?

Well, a good place to start is with an exercise I often do as a coach in strategic planning sessions called "Stop, Start and Continue." Here's how it works. You simply ask yourself these three questions:

- What would I like to *start* doing?
- What would I like to *stop* doing?
- What would I like to *continue* doing?

The answers will then guide you through the process.

Let's break each of the questions down – and assign each of them a James Bond title just for fun.

Question One: What would you like to start doing? Well, how do you want to develop yourself further? Do you want to learn a new skill? Do you want to refresh an old one you had, that you abandoned? Or do you want to focus taking what you already do to a higher level – maybe keep yourself more organized, exercise more, or go back to school to get a higher degree in your field. Think about what you want to bring in to your life that will make it more enjoyable, more productive and/or more satisfying – and then get specific about how you're going to make that happen. Because the answers to this question often prompt significant reinventions, we'll call this category - *You Only Live Twice.*

Question Two: What you like to stop doing? In this category, you can examine any bad habits you have that negatively affect your life.

For example, are you still a smoker, despite all the medical risks that have been proven over the years? Do you find yourself consuming too much alcohol in social situations, which causes you to say and do things that come back to haunt you? Professionally, are you chronically late for meetings and phone calls? Are you working too many hours and finding that your family life is suffering? Look at areas in your life that are lacking and find ways to break out of patterns that are causing problems. Your Bond movie title here? Obviously, *Dr. NO.*

Question Three: What should you continue? This is the best question by far, because here you get to focus on what's going *right* with your life and work – and what you do that creates those positive outcomes. Obviously, these are habits and qualities you want to support, reinforce and even improve on if you can - the "old" parts of you that still have a meaningful contribution to make to your "new" version. They represent the jewels of your life that should always shine bright. In other words, these *Diamonds Are Forever.*

Most of the answers to these three questions have to do with areas that can easily be adjusted – finances, work habits, your health and well-being, etc. What hopefully is consistent in your life are the areas that I consider to be timeless, areas that transcend the old and the new – areas such as your values, your principles, your trustworthiness, your character, your work ethic, and your life attitudes. When these are positive and in place, you'll find the execution of the "Stop, Start and Continue" exercise to be a breeze. If there's a weakness in that list, however, you have some more fundamental work to do on yourself. After all, when all you're doing is chasing money, pleasure and power, you'll find... *The World Is Not Enough.*

(By the way, for those of you who think I'm straying from my superhero theme with this chapter, let me assure you that James Bond is, in fact, a superhero. Show me some other normal guy who could survive everything he has and I'll retract my statement!).

Change and Consistency together dare you to identify what's worth keeping and what's worth improving – and combine them to help create the best version of you. My advice is to do the "Start, Stop and Continue" exercise on an annual basis – and invite trusted mentors, coaches and loved ones to help you out.

After all, this process doesn't have to be...For Your Eyes Only.

DYNAMIC DUO SCORECARD #2

Dynamic Duo:	**Change and Consistency**
Helps You:	**Create Ongoing Self-Improvement**
Obtained by:	**Evaluation and Action**
Brings You:	**Growth and Wisdom**

THOUGHT AND ACTION: THE PB & J OF SUCCESS

Thought and Action. Two other ideas that seem diametrically opposed to each other, like Change and Consistency in our last chapter. But, just like in that case, it turns out we need both of them in our lives.

But there are those who feel differently.

I get a lot of content-driven emails, some I've subscribed to and some that just show up in my in-box. I also subscribe to a lot of blogs. And I read almost all of this stuff, because I like to see what other people are putting out there. Nobody has the market on great ideas, so I think it's important to be exposed to different kinds of thinking.

Every so often, though, one of these blogs or emails will take up an extreme position and, in my opinion, really lose the big picture in the process. Recently, I read two that took completely opposite positions on the topic of this chapter.

The first was all about the power of positive thinking. If you've read everything up until this point, you know I'm a firm believer in this principle – that a winning attitude precedes the actual winning. But this particular writer seemed to think that attitude is where it starts *and* stops – all you have to do is sit in a lotus position and have positive thoughts and you'll get everything you want out of life. Imagine if Superman tried that. Suppose he didn't put on that cape – and, instead, sat around and *thought* about evildoers being defeated. His comic books would, of course, be a lot more boring - except for the surprise ending where the unopposed evildoers take over the world.

Then I read a blog that took the exact opposite position. Positive thinking? Overrated. Maybe even useless. What matters is taking massive action. No mention of having any kind of strategy or thought preceding that action. To me, that's an even more dangerous recipe. Action without thought leads to completely unplanned results. In this scenario, Superman would might go after bad guys and, in the process, level an entire city without a second thought. Not appreciated, Man of Steel.

Ideally, we should be a combination of another dynamic duo – dreamers and doers. That, however, doesn't happen as often as it should, as people tend to be one or the other. The dreamers are great at thinking about what they want out of life – but, when you sit down and talk with them, they'll frequently give you the sense that they think they can't achieve those things. Deep down, they usually think their ambitions are beyond their control – so they end up jumping from dream to dream, dismissing the last one whenever they get tired of failing with it.

The doers? They're all about being busy beavers. They've always got a lot going on and seem to be in a perpetual frenzy. When you talk to the doers about where they're actually going with their lives, however, they're never really sure. They feel like they're going somewhere because they never let up – but, unfortunately, they too often resemble a chicken without its head, furiously running around the barnyard until it exhausts itself.

The 20th Century French philosopher Henri Bergson got it exactly right when he said, "Think like a man of action and act like a man of thought." Or to put it another way, dream in order to do – and do with your dream in mind. Thought and Action go together like another great combination, peanut butter and jelly. They're good individually, but sandwiched together?

Unbeatable.

Ed DeCosta

DYNAMIC DUO SCORECARD #3

Dynamic Duo:	**Thought and Action**
Helps You:	**Achieve Planned Results**
Obtained by:	**Positive Attitude and Directed Deeds**
Brings You:	**Strategic Success**

TIMELESS AND TEMPORARY

Remember when we all used to use those old 5 pound giant cell phones? Now – do you remember what you did with that thing when you upgraded?

I don't know what you do with old gadgets, but I end up throwing them in a drawer and forgetting about them when they've outlived their usefulness. Well, I happened to go through that drawer a few weeks ago and found a cellphone that was about twenty years old. I'll spare you the list of its features, because it's pretty short compared to today's models. The only GPS app it had was… well, it wasn't really an app. Someone just used it once to point me in the direction I should go. At the time I bought this phone, I was incredibly excited at how much it would increase my productivity. Little did I know that today's smartphones would have the computing power to manage a mission to Mars.

Then I stumbled upon a Palm Pilot – a Palm V, the last in the line. This one was over fifteen years old, but, again, it was a thrilling purchase at the time. It had a built-in stylus you could use to write on the device and it had a lot of other features to keep a guy like me organized no matter where I was. Yep, in 1999, a Palm V was cutting-edge *and* expensive – but you can get one now on EBay for the amazing discount price of $9.99 (I checked).

Both of the above two items I've described were, at the time, representatives of breakthrough technology. Back then, I couldn't imagine anything being more sophisticated. But, of course, since that time, there have been literally hundreds and hundreds of new device releases which do thousands and thousands of more things. Now, musicians are able to compose, artists are able to create and filmmakers are able to make entire movies – all on a little ol' iPhone!

And technology continues to march on…

Now, you can either bemoan the fact that you have to replace your devices every time a manufacturer creates a new and innovative model – or you can appreciate the fact that these are only temporary, but valuable, tools that do great things for any business person with a crowded schedule. But one thing you should never do is mistake these gadgets for the timeless tools that are available to us all absolutely free – and never need to be replaced. They make the real difference in taking our lives forward.

Here are two of my favorite timeless tools (and keep in mind you won't find them in an online auction):

1. **Focus.** Concentrate on your highest priorities – and choose those priorities based on a plan of what it is you want to accomplish, what it is you want to be and what you want your life to look like. Keep those things top-of-mind and your priorities should easily fall into place. It's pretty easy to determine whether or not you're focused on the right things: look at what you got done this week, or yesterday, or last week, and ask yourself how in alignment were those achievements with your highest purpose. That's what focus is all about. But to maintain that focus, you need another timeless tool…

2. **Discipline**. Discipline has as its root the Latin word, "disciplina." And you might be surprised to learn that its meaning is "instruction" or "teaching." But when you think about it, it's completely logical – because discipline is actually self-teaching: It's about staying aware of what we're doing and how we're doing it, always with the question in mind, "Is this the best possible choice for me to make right now?" Staying true to making the right choices for the long term is what discipline is all about.

The temporary tools, such as your smartphone or your laptop, are what help you get through the day and navigate your regular work. The timeless tools, however, are what help you get through your *life*. They're internal qualities that never go out of style - and only you can furnish them.

The temporary and the timeless. You need both to become the best version of you.

DYNAMIC DUO SCORECARD #4

Dynamic Duo:	**Timeless and Temporary Tools**
Helps You:	**Reach Short-term and Lifetime Goals**
Obtained by:	**Inner Training – and Outside Purchases**
Makes You:	**Prepared for Life's Challenges**

GOALS AND ROLES

The play's the thing.

Or the movie or the TV show.

In each of these cases, every actor is assigned a different role – a part he or she has to learn and completely understand emotionally in order to play it correctly. If you don't understand where you fit into a production, you'll stick out like a sore thumb – and blunt the effectiveness of how well the story is told. The actor's not the thing – the *play's* the thing. Everybody needs to make their assigned contribution to deliver what's hopefully a memorable experience for the audience.

Well, it's the same thing with any organization, whether it be a business, a government or even the local church, when they're pursuing a group goal. Everyone needs to know their individual roles and fulfill them. If those involved aren't sure what they're supposed to do, the effort turns chaotic and confused.

Whenever I begin working with a company as a coach, I typically like to ask people, "What is your goal, and what is your role?" Both are important to understand – especially what the person's relation is to what the group is trying to accomplish. Who does what – and how does that advance the group's agenda? That's the puzzle that needs to be solved.

Now - think about the group you're in. Do you know its goal – as well as your role in achieving that goal?

Let's look at a very simple example of a group trying to achieve a goal. Think about a group photo you've been a part of at some point in your life. Maybe it's a family photo, maybe it's a sports team photo, maybe it's an office photo. Once the picture has been taken, what's the first think you look at? Obviously, the answer is yourself. That doesn't make you an egomaniac, it just means you want to make sure you didn't screw it up. So you check to make sure your tongue isn't out, your eyes aren't closed, etc. Once you're done looking at your own appearance, then you broaden your perspective and look at everybody else to see how the photo looks as a whole.

That process is very similar to how you should approach your role in a group goal. Your first thought should be directed to how well you're doing your part in it, instead of looking over your shoulder at everybody else. When everybody is concerned with doing their best at what they're supposed to be doing, group goals are so much easier and pleasurable to pursue.

Sports is another great example of what roles and goals are all about. In basketball, for example, the defense is as vital as the offense. Shooting baskets is, of course, the glamourous job, because scoring points visibly puts you ahead of the opposition. But what's just as important is stopping that opposition from scoring more points than you. On a team, everybody plays a huge role – including those who aren't even on the court. A trainer, a coach, even the laundry service that takes care of the uniforms…these are all necessary roles that need to be fulfilled in order for the team to be successful.

Heck, even superheroes need to understand how to work with each other. Suppose you saw an Avengers movie where Thor wasn't thinking straight and threw his hammer right at Captain America's head? Old Cap would see more stars than the ones that happened to be his uniform!

So I challenge you – no matter organization you're involved with – ask your team members, "What is our goal – and what is *my* role?" Make sure everyone's in agreement on the former – and make sure you're up to speed on the latter.

DYNAMIC DUO SCORECARD #5

Dynamic Duo:	**Goals and Roles**
Helps You:	**Understand Your Part in Group Progress**
Obtained by:	**Being on Same Page as Your Partners**
Brings You:	**United and Powerful Group Effort**

PART 5
SAVING THE DAY:
HOW TO BE YOUR OWN
(AND EVERYONE ELSE'S)
HERO

"Nurture your mind with great thoughts. To believe in the heroic makes heroes."

— BENJAMIN DISRAELI

Are you aware that when the ultimate superhero, Superman himself, was first conceived, he couldn't really fly?

It's true. The creators, Jerry Siegel and Joe Shuster, made it so that he could jump pretty high, he was strong enough to pick up a car and thick-skinned enough to not get hurt by a bullet. But that was about it. They originally compared his strength and jumping abilities to that of an ant and a grasshopper. In other words, this Man of Steel began as merely a Bug of Some Consequence.

Today? Superman can fly through space, use his heat vision to melt through walls, use his X-Ray vision to see through walls, fly so fast he can travel through time, etc. etc. etc. As a matter of fact, his powers increased to such a ridiculous extreme over the years that the Superman writers had difficulty thinking up anything that could actually present a challenge to him!

I can't promise you'll make it to that exalted position with your inner superhero, but I'll do what I can.

So far in this book, I've given you the building blocks of becoming a superhero. I've also taught you how to defeat some pretty difficult arch-villains - and uncovered a few powerful dynamic duos that can fight for you in your everyday life.

Now, let's see just how high you can fly.

In the next few chapters, I'm going to share with you some ideas and advice on how to optimize your newfound powers and make the most of them in your professional and personal lives. So get ready to give your new superpowers a test spin – and find out just how much of a hero you can be!

WORST TO FIRST

I hope you'll excuse another mention of my beloved Boston Red Sox – it's only because there's an excellent lesson to learn from these guys. And you don't have to be a fan to know what I'm talking about.

Back in 2012, the team crashed and burned. They won 69 and lost 93, their first losing season in 15 years and their first season in which they lost over 90 games in 46 years. That year, the new manager was fighting with the team most of the time and ended up being fired the day after their last game of the season.

The team executives were determined that 2013 would be a very different story. They hired a new manager, changed the team culture and made some controversial player switches. The fact is that many of the new players the Red Sox acquired were thought to be less talented than some of the ones they had traded away. To seasoned baseball analysts, that spelled trouble for the new season – most picked them to once again finish near the bottom of the standings.

It takes an expert to get it that wrong. Because not only did they finish first in their division, not only did they go on to the play-offs…they won the World Series!

Forgive me, I have to take a moment to calm down from reliving all the excitement. There, that's better.

Going from "worst to first" doesn't happen all that often – and almost never that quickly. But this team did it. And here's one of the secrets behind *how* they did it.

Remember that I mentioned that management changed the team's culture? Well, one of those changes involved one very small thing that made a huge difference.

On the jerseys of a pro baseball team, you'll usually find the name of the club on the front – and the name of the player wearing the jersey on the back. That's the case with most professional sports teams. But, in 2013, the Red Sox changed it up – they removed the players' names from the jerseys, because they wanted to send a strong message both to the players and to the outside world. The message was that these guys were not in it for individual glory, they were there to play as a *team*. The Red Sox management wanted a strong visual reminder that the group goal was more important that each separate player's goals.

I'm not saying that's the only reason they recovered their mojo that year, but I do believe it certainly contributed. The best teams are selfless and think only about finding victory together – and the worst teams are made up of prima donnas who are only in it for themselves. In the latter case, they pull apart instead of pull together – and that affects everyone's attitude.

Think back to the chapter on "Goals and Roles" in the last section of the book – where I talked about how everyone on a team has to understand their specific place in achieving a group goal and follow through on it. That's just what the Red Sox did and it helped guarantee a positive outcome. In these cases, victory does come to the individual – but it also occurs for the entire organization.

Let's go deeper into building a winning team.

When you're hiring or recruiting people to be a part of your organization, what do you look for? You certainly want people with experience and wisdom, especially if they're going to serve in a role of higher responsibility. And of course, they need to have the skills required for whatever job you need done – that's a no-brainer.

But there's something more important than all of the above.

I'm talking about the *quality* of the person. I'm talking about the values and principles by which they live their lives. I'm talking about people who have passion, enthusiasm, courage, integrity and a positive attitude.

You can't teach the above – individuals either possess them or they don't. You can't train someone to be a high quality person, the way you can teach them skills or the ins and outs of the actual job. They either have these values in place or they don't.

So, before you hire someone, make sure you've got a quality person on your hands.

If you simply look for who went to the best college, who has the best connections, the highest IQ or even the highest skill level, you could be in for a rude surprise. It's happened to many a client of mine, when they hired on the basis of what a candidate looked like on paper – and not on the basis of who the candidate really was as a person.

There are very small differences between a business that thrives, one that barely survives and one that doesn't make it. You can have everything you think you need to succeed – and then find that some intangible failure of character and culture continues to sabotage your efforts. Hiring the wrong kind of people can create that negative energy.

My advice is always to hire the best *people*, not the best talents. There's no difference between someone who's great at what he does and only gives 50% - and another person who's half as good and gives 100%. When you do the math, you'll see you get the same results - with a much happier experience.

Building a successful team, however, isn't just about adding the right people. Sometimes it's about subtracting the wrong people.

Many clients who are trying to grow their business, in terms of gaining more revenue, more customers, more profitability and creating a bigger operation, tell me they need to mainly focus on bringing in more people. Their logic is, the more people they have on staff, the more they'll accomplish.

But it can be just as important to weed out those who aren't doing you any favors.

Here's a simple exercise you can do to discover if you're in this position. Get a complete list of all your employees and go through those names one-by-one. As you go through the list, imagine if each person on it resigned – not all at once of course, but just the particular name you've landed on at the moment.

Now...what would your reaction be to that person's resignation? Would it be a panicked...

"What am I going to do? She's invaluable!"

Or would it be a more measured...

"Oh, I like him. Too bad, but it won't be hard to replace him."

Or would it simply be...

A huge sigh of relief and a whoop of joy.

It sounds cruel, but, at most companies, there are at least a few people whose resignation would result in that very truthful and telling last reaction. Why? Because, for whatever reason, they can't or won't do their jobs – or their personality is such that they prevent others from doing theirs. Maybe they cause internal problems, such as political infighting or bickering, maybe they engage in destructive gossip, or maybe they treat co-workers or, worse yet, customers in rude and abusive ways.

More often than not, these kinds of employees cause more problems than they solve – if they're solving any at all. Again, this may sound cruel and I certainly don't mean to be flip about this kind of difficult situation, but you owe it to the rest of your employees as well as the overall organization to get rid of people who are disrupting the operation.

The truth is, you're doing these people a favor when you respectfully release them from their positions. When you go about it in a way that's moral and ethical (and yes, legal), it can be a wake-up call they'll never forget. You might even hear down the line, maybe not even firsthand but through the grapevine, that this was the best thing to ever happen to them. Often, they're trapped in a negative pattern that perpetuates itself – and, as part of that pattern, you're unwittingly aiding and abetting it.

And, by the way, this can happen in your personal life as well. Yes, there will be people in your life you love to have around, but there will also be people who pull you down and cause emotional havoc. If that's the case with you, if there are those who bring more darkness than light into your life, consider revoking their privileges to take up your time and drain your energy.

To sum up, you can create addition with subtraction. As a matter of fact, it's a necessary task that has to be done every so often by all of us – so don't let guilt or a false sense of responsibility prevent you from taking an action that's best for everyone.

One final thought on what it takes to raise a team to hero status – and it's about what style of leadership is most effective.

One of the most insightful comments I ever heard from Dr. Martin Luther King was genuine leaders are not searchers for consensus, but *molders* of consensus. I really saw that illustrated when I recently worked with a corporate leadership team. I can't reveal the identity of the company, but I will say that I was there to help the team create a list of priorities. The team was wildly successful, but they were beginning to try and do everything at once.

Where the head of this team excelled was in molding a consensus.

He didn't make the mistake of telling everybody what to do, like a dictatorial person might. Now, of course, a dictatorship can seem very efficient. One person makes all the decisions, gives out all the orders and everyone just needs to comply. But it's certainly not efficient in the long run and I'll tell you why: Because people don't buy in. They don't contribute ideas, their hearts aren't in it and they end up going through the motions. When people don't feel like they're part of the decision-making process, they're not truly engaged in the company's well-being. Something is lost.

The head of the team also didn't make the mistake of simply taking a vote on what to do. Leadership isn't just about handing out surveys and using the outcome as a basis for a plan of action. That's what Dr. King meant by *searching* for consensus. A leader has to be more than a delegate of the team – he or she has to truly lead the team and guide them to the best possible solutions, not the most popular ones.

Instead of making either of those mistakes, the head of the team listened to the group, found the areas where they had common ground and brought them together in agreement on how to move forward as a team. That involved a lot of listening and sharing. Even when you have the most cohesive leadership team in the world, it still includes people who have different perspectives, different agendas and disparate views of what needs to be done. It's up to the leader to process all this feedback, repeat it back to the team and put it all together to form a coherent and effective plan.

By molding consensus, there are ways to accomplish almost everyone's objectives together. I say "almost," because there are always instances where one or two opinions clearly don't resonate with the group – but that comes after a fair and full hearing where everyone gets to speak their minds. Even though a few people's thoughts may not be a part of the end product, they can still feel as though they were a part of the process. And hopefully, they won't view the outcome as a personal defeat – but as a collective win for the group. Everyone put their heads together, shared openly, honestly and even emotionally, and a strategy was forged from that.

It takes real leadership to transport your group to a productive and positive destination. It takes molding a consensus.

SUPER SCORECARD #13

Superpower:	**Building a Powerful Team**
Allows you to:	**Successfully Strategize and Achieve Goals**
Obtained by:	**Assembling the Right People and Leading Them**
Arch Enemy:	**Unproductive Leadership Principles**

DOING THE IMPOSSIBLE

The Roman Emperor Marcus Aurelius was that rare political leader who actually said things that make sense.

I kid, but Aurelius, who ruled around 2000 years ago, was responsible for many memorable quotes that have stood the test of time. And one of my favorites is this:

"Because a thing seems difficult for you, do not think it impossible for anyone to accomplish."

If you're truly after attaining heroic status, the above words should never be far from your thoughts.

The history books are full of examples of people achieving feats that others were convinced couldn't be done. Most of you have heard of Roger Bannister, the great track athlete who, in 1954, broke the four-minute mile barrier. The nine years before that, no one set a new world record in running the mile. Even doctors were saying that running the mile in four minutes was physically impossible. But Bannister did it – and, as soon as he did, other runners quickly began breaking *his* record. When Bannister proved that running that fast was not impossible, it became obvious that the real block to progress had been psychological, not physical. Today, as I write this, Bannister's record has been beat by over 16 seconds; that would put Bannister 125 yards back when the latest record holder crossed the finish line – he would be behind the frontrunner by over the length of a football field.

Of course, there are many other dramatic instances of accomplishing great things that, in the past, had been thought to be impossible. Airplanes, heart transplants, the moon landing, television, even personal computers. To those living 150 years ago, all of these would seem like miracles.

How do you achieve the impossible in your life?

First of all, you have to set aggressive goals that go beyond your comfort zone - and beyond conventional thinking. Set goals even though you may not have any idea of how to achieve them at this moment – then think and act as if you are certain you will achieve them.

It's a process I call CBA – Conceive, Believe and Achieve.

When you know in your gut you can do something that others say can't be done, that's the optimum time to put CBA to work. Whether it's a matter of your physical fitness, your business life, your finances, or some other aspect of your life you're concerned about, set that aggressive goal. Be firm in your belief that you can achieve it – and then quickly take action. When you combine firm conviction with targeted action, you can reach an "impossible" goal.

Here's the thing about the word, "impossible." Inside of it, you'll find two other words – "I'm possible."

Now, let's talk about the timetable for getting the impossible done.

For that, let's turn from the Marcus Aurelius quote I cited earlier to some lyrics from an old Billie Holiday standard, "Crazy He Calls Me," which states:

"The difficult I'll do right now, the impossible may take a little while."

In other words, when you do attempt the impossible, the quality you may be most in need of is *patience*.

As Emperor Aurelius would no doubt verify if he were around today, Rome wasn't built in a day. Building something lasting and awesome takes time. One of Aesop's most famous fables was "The Tortoise and the Hare." It has a lasting power for a reason, especially in today's world, where we're surrounded by devices that heighten the speed of everything.

Remember when you actually had to go get photos developed? Now they appear fully-formed in the blink of an eye – and on your phone. Remember when you had to wait a few days to get a letter in the mail? Now, it appears in your in-box faster than it would take you to walk to your mailbox.

Modern life continues to get faster and faster – and that tends to make us more and more impatient to get things done. But Aesop's wisdom from centuries ago still resonates: Slow and steady wins the race. That means if you had a good day yesterday, it doesn't matter – that was then, this is now, so keep working hard and working smart again today. If you had a bad day yesterday, it also doesn't matter – forget about those setbacks and keep pressing forward *today*. Consistent effort is the key.

Eventually, the consistent effort pays off in creating momentum, the Big Mo, which generates its own special brand of excitement and energy. It's the feeling that makes you want to yell "I got this!" - because you feel success is just around the corner.

But, again, it takes time to build that kind of momentum

The idea of the overnight success is almost entirely a myth. Generally, what the term really means is that a person (or a business) has worked very hard for a very long time to reach a critical moment of amazing success – a success that captures the public's attention. When that happens, people can't accept the fact that they haven't heard of this person prior to that time. Therefore – that person must have just created their success out of thin air in an instant! Of course, that's not the truth – which is that their efforts over the long haul were what prepared them to leap into the spotlight and dazzle everyone in sight. An "overnight" success takes years and years to bring fame to fruition.

So stay patient – and stay focused. Yesterday ended last night. No matter what your results were then, you still have to keep moving forward today. If you can keep on keeping on, you will live your own Impossible Dream.

And you probably won't ever want to wake up from it.

SUPER SCORECARD #14

Superpower:	**Doing the "Impossible"**
Allows you to:	**Reach Extremely Difficult, Rewarding Goals**
Obtained by:	**Time, Patience and Continual Exertion**
Arch Enemy:	**Erratic Unfocused Effort**

MY FAVORITE PALINDROME

Racecar.
Dr. Awkward.
Evil Olive.
Madam Adam.
What do these words have in common? They're all palindromes.

If you don't know what a palindrome is, I'll tell you (I do try to be helpful). It's a word, phrase or sentence that, when spelled forward or backwards, is the same. The above four palindromes I just listed are ones I remember from when I was a little kid.

You can do a lot with palindromes. You can title a book: *A Man, A Plan, A Canal: Panama.* You can ask a question: "Are we not drawn onward to new era?" Or you can make a judgment about some individuals: Dennis, Nell, Edna, Leon, Nedra, Anita, Rolf, Nora, Alice, Carol, Leo, Jane, Reed, Dena, Dale, Basil, Rae, Penny, Lana, Dave, Denny, Lena, Ida, Bernadette, Ben, Ray, Lila, Nina, Jo, Ira, Mara, Sara, Mario, Jan, Ina, Lily, Arne, Bette, Dan, Reba, Diane, Lynn, Ed, Eva, Dana, Lynne, Pearl, Isabel, Ada, Ned, Dee, Rena, Joel, Lora, Cecil, Aaron, Flora, Tina, Arden, Noel, and Ellen sinned.

You'll notice the name "Ed" was not in the above list.

The longer the palindrome is, the more impressive it is. But my favorite one is pretty short – and it doesn't even spell out an actual word. It's an acronym.

Here it is:
DWYSYWD

I first discovered this palindrome when my brother Jim emailed me about 15 years ago – and I noticed he had it placed in his signature line. I stared at it, trying to figure out what it was. It seemed like it would have something to do with where he worked, but it didn't seem to relate to his company or his title, it was too long for that. But I couldn't for the life of me figure out what it meant, even though I know my brother Jim pretty well – after all, he's my brother.

And then it dawned on me.

DWYSYWD - "Do What You Say You Will Do."

I called him to make sure I was guessing right – and turned out I had the right answer. I'll spare you the details of why he was putting it on all his emails at the time, but I won't skip over why this acronym is vital to your superhero status.

You see, DWYSYWD is fundamental to building and maintaining the strongest possible relationships, both in your personal and professional lives.

Relationships, of course, are rooted in trust. The more each person trusts the other, the closer the relationship becomes. When you know you can truly rely on the other person's word, it takes a huge weight off your shoulders.

That all springs from each person in the relationship doing what they say they'll do.

Of course, there are a lot of other things we all do to build and maintain trust – but following the principle of DWYSYWD is a wonderful start. It's as simple as calling when you say you're going to call, or taking action on a project you promised to follow through on. You don't necessarily have to do more than you say you're going to do, although that's always nice. Just do what you say you will.

So practice DWYSYWD in order to build rich and rewarding relationships with those you love and those you work with. It's an easy way to be a hero – and you'll end up having a lot of people in your live who trust you...well, forwards and backwards.

SUPER SCORECARD #15

Superpower:	Matching Words with Action
Allows you to:	Build Strong Relationships
Obtained by:	Follow Through
Arch Enemy:	Inconsistency and Broken Promises

HOW DO YOU TOLE-RATE?

The sad truth is even superheroes don't always get along.

There's always a scene in one of the Avengers movies where one of the gang bashes on another (I hate to point fingers, but the Hulk is generally the guilty party). The result? Superheroes end up getting thrown through walls, knocking down buildings and cracking streets in half.

It really ends up punishing the taxpayers, let's face it. And it's hard to believe that self-avowed heroes who have pledged to defend the world can't avoid these petty squabbles – but it's true. The ultimate evidence is a little movie entitled *Batman v. Superman*. I mean, if the original superhero twosome can't break bread together, what hope is there for the world?

Well, there's actually a lot of hope for the real world – the one without costumed superheroes – if we would all just make the effort to get along.

Superheroes may need conflict to make a good story, but, frankly, we don't. As a matter of fact, we can create amazing outcomes if we avoid a tussle and instead try to cooperate. And that's where the title of this chapter comes into play.

How *do* you tole-rate?

In other words, when you meet up with those who are different than you, how willing are you to accept those differences rather than condemn them?

As an executive coach, I find myself interacting with organizations of all shapes and sizes. I deal with various industries and various cultures, located not just all over the country, but all over the world. So, of course, it's natural that I end up encountering people who have many differences of opinion – not only with me, but with one another. Notice I used the word, "natural." We're all individuals, we all come from different places, and we all have different ways of thinking – and that's okay.

What's not okay is letting those differences of opinion get in the way of cooperation and collaboration within whatever organization to which they belong. Intolerance hurts any group effort and, to be blunt, it hurts the people who are insistent on their way being the correct one.

And, when the Hulk is involved, it also really hurts the building he happens to be punching.

Tolerance is definitely a super-power you need to take on board if you're going to perform great feats. And here are three "A" words that will help you increase your own tole-rate score:

1. Acknowledge

Tolerance starts by simply acknowledging the fact, as I've just stated, that differences of opinion are very natural in the world. If everybody was right about everything, we'd spend our days just nodding at each other.

Would it really be better if we were a planet full of Yes Men and Yes Women, acting like clones of each other? Absolutely not. We might get a lot more done, but the world in turn would be a much weirder and more boring world. Not only that, progress would be almost unattainable, simply because everyone thought the same way. In contrast, diversity of thought tends to breed more creativity, innovative ideas and breakthrough initiatives.

Our differences actually make us stronger. And we all need to remember that, especially when we're watching cable news.

2. Accept

After you acknowledge people's differences, you must then accept and even welcome those with varying opinions on politics, religion, business and life. These include people who live very different lives than you do. Now, this doesn't mean you have to hang out with murderers and invite thieves to dinner (if you do, hide the jewelry). But you should seek to understand and be comfortable with those with different belief systems than you.

To do that, practice building your empathy skills; instead of engaging in an instant argument, ask questions and try to determine who they are, what they're about and where they're coming from. How did they come to think the way they do? Why are they very passionate about certain viewpoints? Don't walk into this kind of conversation automatically assuming your job is to change their attitudes – just settle for understanding them.

3. Agree

If you have to work with someone whose personal views are diametrically opposed to yours, then…agree.

I don't mean agree with their views, but agree on the fact that none of your opinions should get in the way of the task at hand. You can absolutely work closely and wonderfully with an aggressive atheist even if you're a conservative Christian. Or with a liberal left-winger if you're a diehard Republican. Or with a devoted vegan you're your favorite food is a double bacon cheeseburger. Here's the bottom line: The things that usually cause conflicts between co-workers very often have *absolutely nothing to do with what both of you are supposed to be doing together.*

Don't misunderstand me. I would never suggest you abandon your beliefs or even back down from them because of another person. What I *do* advocate is that you agree to disagree and find common ground about how to move forward. You can even joke about your differences of opinion if that works for both of you – as long as each person is respectful of the other and stays away from serious debates involving any subject that's laden with landmines.

What matters is *what matters* – and that's usually about what has to get done, not who either one of you is supporting in the next election.

As we come to the close of this chapter, I'm going to cop to some intolerance of my own.

I was very unfair to the Avengers earlier.

Now, I don't admit to this simply because most of them could tear me apart limb from limb (although that would definitely be a consideration if any of these guys actually existed). I say this because when you consider who actually makes up this super group - a Norse God, a billionaire industrialist, a super-soldier from World War II, and a giant green monster with a very limited vocabulary, among others – it's amazing they even can get through a meeting without leveling the place. So, if they engage in the occasional brawl, who am I to judge them?

Here's the way to look at it, from my point of view: If this strange collection of multicolored men can put aside their differences to save the world...well, you can get along with somebody who believes goldfish talk to him long enough to get a job done.

As long as that goldfish isn't talking trash about you, of course.

SUPER SCORECARD #16

Superpower:	Tolerance
Allows you to:	Forge Alliances with Different Kinds of People
Obtained by:	Acceptance and Having an Open Mind
Arch Enemy:	Prejudice and Narrow-mindedness

CALL YOUR MOM!

As I write this, I've been rocked by two very unexpected tragedies.

The first was a car accident in our area involving three young people – all college-aged students. Two out of three are out of the hospital and the third looks like he will have a full recovery and be home with his family soon.

The second was another car accident, involving a friend of mine, a fellow coach named Kirk. He wasn't so lucky and passed away. I'm still stunned by his sudden death as are all of his friends.

Life is fragile, friends. You never know.

In my role as a business coach, I try to help people boost their productivity to the limit. I want my clients to seize the day – you know, all that carpe diem stuff Robin Williams talked about in the movie, *Dead Poets' Society*. It's my job. And I apply that same advice to myself. I want to make the most of each hour and realize the most results possible.

But both of the recent incidents I briefly described at the beginning of this chapter have motivated me to slow down a little.

Too many of us run around trying to do too much too fast. I can be guilty of this same crime. "Stop and smell the roses" is a cliché for a reason, as most clichés are – it contains more than a kernel of truth. When we're rushing through our days, we lose appreciation for all that we have and all there is to enjoy. Without that appreciation – without that enjoyment – it can be tempting to say, "What's the point?" And that just leads to classic burn-out.

That's why, now that we're at the end of this section of the book, I'd like to offer what I consider to be a very heroic challenge.

In the next few minutes, get in touch with a few people that you love – and tell them you love them.

If they're physically accessible, tell them face-to-face and give them a big hug. Make sure they understand how you feel about them. If they're not, then call them and tell them. Don't text them a smiley-face. That won't do the job.

Here are two more challenges for you.

Smile. Enjoy the day.

You don't think those two challenges are hard? You'd be amazed at how many people have difficulty with them. They're sentiments that pop up on office posters, kitchen magnets and social media posts on a regular basis. And the reason for that is a little sad.

We actually have to be *reminded* to enjoy our lives.

Look, none of us knows how much time we're going to have on this earth – or how much time our loved ones will have, hard as that is to consider. And what I'm about to say will sound contrary to a lot of the messages I've been delivering in this book. But sometimes it isn't about working harder or faster in order to get more done.

Sometimes…you just have to *live*.

I believe passionately in planning and adhering to long-term strategies. But I also believe in enjoying today.

So let me offer a few more challenges…

Take a walk with your significant other.

Let your parents or grandparents, if they're alive, know that you love them and that you appreciate them.

If there's anyone that you owe an apology to, call them and say, "I'm sorry." Don't wait.

Now, flip that around. Is there someone who owes you an apology? Someone who you should've forgiven by now for whatever offense or transgression they committed against you? Then don't hold a grudge.

Let it go. Call them and let them off the hook, even if you were right and they were dead wrong. Life's too short.

And I mean that. There's a never a day that goes by when there aren't obituaries in the newspaper. And when people die, it's a tragedy, even if we don't happen to know the deceased - someone is still affected by that death. When we happen to know that someone, we send our condolences – and also maybe flowers, or a donation to the deceased's favorite charity. But when we do that, it's almost an automatic impulse - we're too often going through the motions. We don't understand that one day it's going to be us in one of those obituaries – and that will be the day when we can no longer tell those we love how we feel, when we can no longer forgive those we should, when we can no longer enjoy the things in life we take for granted.

So…take advantage of today. Relish it. If you know someone who's lonely or needs a tender touch, reach out to them. Don't put it off until next week or next month when you have more time. Do it now.

You'll be glad you did.

Oh – and like the title of this chapter, says…call your mom!

SUPER SCORECARD #17

Superpower:	**Gratitude**
Allows you to:	**Appreciate Your Life**
Obtained by:	**Remembering and Acknowledging All You Have**
Arch Enemy:	**Indifference**

PART 6
SUPER SUCCESS:
FLYING HIGH AND
ENJOYING THE VIEW

"Being a superhero is a lot of fun."

– CHRIS "THOR" HEMSWORTH

There's a scene that happens in most superhero movies where our cos-tumed crusader first obtains his powers – and joyously takes them for a spin. Whether it's Peter Parker scurrying up a wall or an armored Tony Stark jetting around in the sky, you see the excitement in the eyes of someone who was merely human a few minutes ago suddenly realizing he can do things nobody else can.

That's what it feels like when you first release *your* superhero. You may not be able to fly or break through walls - but you most likely will be able to achieve results you never dreamt possible.

So, call this next section "Counseling for Superheroes." The follow-ing chapters are aimed at enhancing your all-powerful experience as an official Ed DeCosta-trained mighty person.

After all, even superheroes need a little care and feeding…

WINNERS HAVE COACHES

Name the best athlete in any given sport.

As a matter of fact, name your favorite athlete in all the sports you enjoy following. Make a list.

Examine your list and think about what these gifted and talented people, people who perform at the very height of their powers, have in common, besides their exceptional skill in what they do.

Here's the one big thing they share: They all have coaches. *Multiple* coaches.

I remind you of the obvious simply because there is the mistaken belief that, once you've become successful in whatever field you happen to compete in, that you're done. You've made it. You have nothing more to learn and you have no room to improve.

Wrong.

The truth is this: *Winners have coaches.*

One of the biggest takeaways you can gain from life is...it's never over. You have to continue to adapt and grow, or, eventually, you start sliding backwards. Your knowledge and abilities atrophy. You lose track of current trends in your business.

That's why you must continue to hone your skills and learn new ones. And that's what coaches help you do - even if you're already feeling like you're a superhero.

Of course, many people don't really understand what a coach like myself, who operates outside of the athletic arena, does. Many think a coach is only there to tell a client what to do. Therefore, it makes sense that if you're successful at what you do, you don't believe you need to be instructed by anyone any longer.

Well, a coach isn't about instruction. A coach is about *improvement.*

Let's go back to the example of a top athlete – let's say for the sake of argument, a major league pitcher. A pro pitcher doesn't have to be told how to throw a curve ball or a slider. He doesn't have to be trained to pick off a runner at first base or avoid committing a balk on the mound during a game. If he didn't already know all that, he wouldn't be in the majors.

No, the reason he needs a coach is to spot when he's unknowingly changed his movement as he throws the ball – which in turn causes a pitch to go off the mark. Or help him as he grows older to make up for his lost pitch speed with smarter throwing strategies. A coach can help the pitcher with any number of things – because the coach can watch the pitcher in a way the pitcher can't do himself. He can supply an objective perspective on how the pitcher does his job and offer ways to improve performance.

It's no different with a business coach.

When you're in the middle of a 24/7 executive job or any kind of demanding career, it's easy to get off-track – or be unable to see how to climb to new levels of achievement. When you get caught up in the day-to-day, it's quite easy to lose sight of that all-important big picture. That's where my other coaching colleagues and I come into play. We help our clients see where they are and where they want to go – and then we assist them with their ambitions.

We're not teachers. Our clients are beyond being students. They're professionals – and they know the value of investing in coaching services to help them improve. The feedback I get in terms of the return on that investment is that, as a result, my clients become better communicators, better leaders and more effective in their working (and even personal) lives. These are all extremely tangible benefits that go right towards bolstering their organizations' bottom lines – and spring directly from these people's innate talents. I just help direct them so they can reap these benefits.

I'd like to offer further insight into what a coach should deliver to a client. Again, according to what my clients have told me over the years, these are the three biggest rewards consistent coaching has granted them:

1. Awareness

Awareness may not sound like the greatest thing since sliced bread, but it's an essential quality to have if you're serious about performing at your highest level. When you're aware of who you are, what your strengths are, what your purpose is and what your role inside the company is, you can feel more confident and focused in how you approach your work. You can also be honest with yourself about your limitations and how to address them.

If you're sleepwalking through your work day, however, all of the above will be a lot more difficult, if not impossible. A coach will always be your wake-up call to ask you direct questions about your mindset and activities - and work with you to find the most honest, valid answers.

2. Intentionality

From a foundation of awareness, a coach will now assist you in addressing the question of where your intentions really lie. Where do you want to go from where you are? What strengths, assets and resources can you utilize to take you from where you are to where you want to be? To take your organization to where you want it to be? Your confidential conversations with a coach can take you through a process of ongoing discovery about those intentions, and help you set realistic goals on a firm timetable, so you know what you want to achieve in a given, day, week, month, quarter or year. A coach will help you align intentions and priorities in a definitive plan that will continue to deliver dividends.

3. Accountability

We've all heard the well-known saying, "The road to hell is paved with good intentions." And there's a certain truth to that if good intentions are the only ingredient in the equation. Intentionality is wonderful, but essentially meaningless if it's not followed up with action. Now, a coach isn't the person who needs to take that action – no coach is going to do the work for you. No, the coach's role is hold you *accountable*.

I've already referenced the power of having an accountability partner. Well, a coach is the ultimate accountability partner – because we're trained to serve that function. Sometimes we'll use carrots, sometimes we'll use sticks – but in most cases, we'll try to put into action a combination of positive and negative reinforcement in order to help our clients attain what they intend to attain. It often all comes down to, "Do you do what you'll say you'll do?" (a question we discussed in an earlier chapter). If you're going to firmly establish trust and build on your ability to lead and influence those around you, the answer to that question has to be "Yes."

Awareness, intentionality and accountability – those are the three big pillars of a successful coaching relationship, as well as the keys to ongoing improvement. You certainly can be happy with your current performance. But if you want to really unlock your potential, look for a coach with whom you can easily communicate and who has a background that's consistent with yours.

By the way, I'm not suggesting everyone needs a coach – but I do believe everyone can benefit from the coaching process. Of course, you can get lots of great self-improvement tips and guidance from books, audio programs, videos and other informational products. Those are all awesome resources and I tap into them myself.

But there's one other important facet of one-on-one coaching that you can't get from digesting premade materials – and that's represented in the words "one-on-one."

All those books, audio CDs and videos are made for the masses – with a one-size-fits-all approach that gives you useful advice, but really can't deal with your specific situation. Even this book, proud as I am of it, can only take you so far.

A coach, in contrast, does nothing *but* deal with your specific situation. He or she can help you customize generic concepts to your own particular needs – and of course, help you progress through the awareness, intentionality and accountability phases. A coach is an experienced advocate for you and your ambitions and works to help you reach those ambitions.

We started this chapter talking about what coaches do for athletes and I'd like to close with a specific and awesome example of that.

Remember Michael Phelps, the Olympic swimmer and most decorated Olympic athlete of all time (22 medals in all)? Well, a coach took him to those heights of success - a man named Bob Bowman. Bowman charted out Phelps' progress for 12 long years before the Olympiad got to the Olympics. Phelps had the talent – but Bowman had the plan, and Phelps knew it.

The proof of that is in a famous photo of Phelps and Bowman, taken just after Phelps broke a record at a swimming event. Phelps, who is literally still dripping wet, is staring at Bowman as he demonstrates to the swimmer how he should adjust an arm movement next time he does an event.

Yes – the coach of the athlete who just broke a record is still working on improving the guy's performance.

And that's what coaching is all about.

SUPER SCORECARD #18

Superpower: Improving Performance

Allows you to: Continue to Grow and Achieve

Obtained by: Being Open to Constructive Coaching

Arch Enemy: Arrogance and Belief that You Know Everything

LIGHTEN UP!

A real superhero always needs a little humor in his or her life.
You'll notice that almost all superheroes have a wisecrack at the ready along with whatever other powers they possess - Robert Downey Jr. as Iron Man is a prime example of that. He quips as he flies into battle because life can be pretty tough – and a little laughter helps even the most super among us get through the day.

So...lighten up. Smile. Laugh. Don't be so serious, especially about yourself.

Yes, we've talked a lot in this book about the importance of being goal-oriented and focusing on performance, all of that great stuff coaches like me enjoy driving home. All of that advice, however, is only about *what* we're doing.

Humor is about *how* we do it. Do you want to trudge through difficulties and necessary tasks feeling down and out – or would you rather make all that as easy to deal with as possible by having a little fun along the way?

Back to our superheroes. They may be wisecracking while they're battling bad guys – but at no moment in the story are they taking their responsibilities any less seriously. When you're in a life-or-death battle to save the world, you have to get your jollies any way you can. And just because Captain America throws out a joke almost as often as he tosses his shield doesn't mean he's any less committed to prevailing over the forces of evil.

Just as a jesting Avenger makes an action scene more enjoyable to watch, a few innocent jokes can immensely improve an average work day. If you're completely grim and all business when you're going about your duties, people won't necessarily jump up and down in excited anticipation when you enter a room. Nor will they turn their frowns upside down – but, instead, they'll keep them firmly in place.

With humor? Even if you're delivering bad news, it goes down a lot easier if you have a sense of humor about it. A spoonful of sugar, as Mary Poppins used to say...

Now, just to be clear, I'm not saying you have to become the next Jimmy Fallon. Nor do you have to put on a big fake red nose and play the clown. You don't want to be Bozo – but you also don't want to be the person who sucks the air out of the room.

You just want to be light-hearted. You want to be serious about your objectives – but willing to have fun on the way to those objectives.

How does humor help in a conversation? Well, think about it. When you see an old friend, you almost immediately go to things you used to laugh about. And when you meet new people, you almost always make obvious jokes about the weather or another common situation that's begging to be made fun of. Why? Because it loosens things up – it makes the other people involved feel warmer and more comfortable and creates a solid bond. Even when people are a bad mood or going through a difficult time, a joke can often bring them out of a funk.

The Reader's Digest wasn't wrong when it proclaimed laughter as the best medicine. Humor takes the tension out of the room. It helps build rapport with people you've never met before. It helps them understand you better and deepens their perspective of who you are. What do I mean by that? Well, when you're comfortable with who you are, you have an easier time laughing about yourself and making self-deprecating jokes. To other people, you appear to be so confident in your own skin that you're not afraid to make fun of yourself.

Contrast that with somebody who's uptight – somebody who either doesn't get a joke or doesn't want to. You deliver a punch line to them and they look at you like you're crazy. Frankly, you have to watch what you say to people like that because they're usually very insecure and will react stone-faced to a little humor. Characters like that are usually made the butt of the joke in TV situation comedies – but are far from fun in real life.

Humor really comes in handy if you've made a mistake or something has unexpectedly gotten screwed up. It helps others (and yourself) get over the initial shock of the setback and move on from it. And it makes everybody feel better about working on a solution to the problem rather than fixating on the reasons things went south in the first place. Stuff happens. A little laughter helps you deal with it.

And, again, in terms of your career as well as leading and influencing others, humor goes a long way to making people want to do business with you, inside and outside your organization. Strangely enough, humor, when used correctly, makes you more likeable and trustworthy than a stiff in a suit that acts like a robot programmed for business.

In the words of the late great Speaker of the House of Representatives, "Tip" O'Neill, "A good lesson in keeping your perspective is: Take your job seriously but don't take yourself seriously." You don't want to try too hard to be a nightclub comic – and you want to make sure a situation is appropriate for humor – but there's no harm and a great deal of benefit to using humor judiciously and properly.

No kidding.

SUPER SCORECARD #19

Superpower: **Sense of Humor**
Allows you to: **Bond with Others, Enjoy a Difficult Day**
Obtained by: **Having a Light Heart**
Arch Enemy: **Overseriousness**

PLANNED SPONTANEITY

The title of this chapter is what's known as an oxymoron – a word or phrase that seems to directly contradict itself, like the phrase, "jumbo shrimp." Just because something is an oxymoron, however, doesn't mean it can't exist. I mean, jumbo shrimp is a definite thing – I've eaten them myself, so I know they're out there. So I hope you'll believe me when I tell you that planned spontaneity is also a thing.

Let me explain.

Most of the ideas I've talked about in this book regarding planning and creating goals that directly pertain to your professional life. But it's important to pay attention to your personal life as well. That point was driven home this past week when a few of my clients happened to mention their upcoming family vacations – you know, the usual one-to-two week trips that need to be nailed down months in advance. Those are the kind of family activities that *have* to be planned - you have to book airline tickets if you're flying, make sure you can get the weeks off you're looking for and make a reservation at the place where you want to stay, among other details. It's awfully hard to book these things at the last minute, especially if they fall in the summer or during the holidays when everybody's taking time off.

That got me to thinking about family events that usually *don't* get planned – the smaller and possibly more important personal get-togethers that enable you to not only preserve but strengthen your ties with loved ones throughout the year. Unfortunately, because they aren't planned, many times they never happen – which causes those relationships to often grow distant and even rupture.

That's something I never wanted to have happen on my end. As most of my clients know, I make it a point to have a one-on-one dinner with each of my three kids on a monthly basis. I also plan a regular date night with my beautiful wife. When I mentioned all this to a client, his reply was, "I'm not big on planning those sorts of things. I'm really more spontaneous, fly-by-the-seat-of-my-pants. I like to do things on a whim."

Well, that's fine if you actually do end up doing them. But when you're busy with your work and other life responsibilities, it's way too easy *not* to do them, because they're simply not a part of your regular schedule. That's why I like to advocate planning in advance to make sure you get the quality time you need with the people you care about. The thing is you can have those plans in place – and still have the flexibility to change the "where" and the "when" of those plans.

For example, my wife and I schedule our regular date night every other Saturday night. That doesn't go away, because we know it's important to make time to keep our relationship alive and thriving. Now, occasionally, one or both of us end up with something else we have to do on a scheduled date night.

What do we do when that happens?

We don't cancel - we reschedule. And we don't limit the date night to the typical dinner and a movie if it doesn't work out. Believe it or not, we've actually made a date night out of going to the grocery store! No, it's not the most romantic date night you can have - but, on the other hand, if it's something you don't regularly do as a couple, it can still be very enjoyable. For instance, you can play kickball with a kumquat in the produce section.

(Note to reader: We didn't really do this, but it's fun to think about.)

Hopefully, you see what I'm getting at here. If you make a date night or a dinner with a child an ongoing item in your schedule, then, in your mind, you're committing to making that happen one way or the other. Same with simple stuff like calling a beloved relative or good friend on a regular basis, which you can easily fit into your day when the time opens up.

If you have a busy schedule, these things generally don't get done - unless they are, in fact, a *part* of your busy schedule. None of these things have to be a big production – but they're worth the effort to make them happen, even if the date, time and venue end up changing at the last minute. The point of it all is to *make it work*. It shows the people involved that you care about them and you're going to make the effort.

And, hey, it's good for you too. These special times give you room to breathe and shift gears, which is always good for your mindset – especially if you keep in mind that these should be enjoyable, informal occasions, where you can have casual conversations without pressure.

Oxymoron or not, I'm a big fan of planned spontaneity. And I'm not just being deceptively honest either.

SUPER SCORECARD #20

Superpower:	**Planned Spontaneity**
Allows you to:	**Keep Family Relations Strong**
Obtained by:	**Scheduling Regular Get-Togethers**
Arch Enemy:	**Taking Family for Granted**

HAPPINESS IS A STATE OF MIND

D o you love your life?

Yes, it's a simple question – but, man, it's a very profound one as well. And many seem to struggle when they have to answer it.

They say things like…

"Well, yes, but…"

"I do love my life…however…"

"Things are going really well…but I have to say…"

Yes, most people want to *say* they love their lives – but they invariably can't help but add a qualifier. They can't seem to just flat-out love their lives. Call them commitment-phobes if you want, but they either want to live somewhere else, be doing something else for a living, find a more fulfilling relationship…

…or even just drive a better car.

In the words of that wise old sage, Rosanne Rosannadanna, "It's always something."

I believe the reason most can't just say they love their lives is they're confused. By what? By the fact that they believe that they're not allowed to fully appreciate their lives – unless those lives are absolutely perfect in every way. Ah, yes, perfection. The goal which none of us can ever fully achieve.

Is that lack of perfection holding you back from appreciating all you do have? From completely enjoying every day you have on planet earth?

If that's the way you feel, then consider these questions…

- Do you love your kids – even though they left a mess in the kitchen?
- Do you love your dog – even after the mutt munched on the carpet?
- Do you love your significant other – even if your beloved forgot to pick up that gallon of milk on the way home like you asked them to?

I'm willing to bet your answer in all of the above cases (unless you don't have a dog, children or a significant other) is YES. You love them all without any disclaimers – even though, undoubtedly, none of them are perfect.

So why does your life have to be perfect?

A while back, I was in California on vacation with my family. We were doing the Hollywood thing, driving by the homes of the stars and we were just knocked out by how huge some of them were. At one point, I turned to my daughter and asked her, "Would you ever want to live in a house like that?" She replied, "For a week, yeah. But actually live in one? Absolutely not."

As we talked more about what the perfect-sized house would be, I felt proud of my girl because she knew how much was enough. A lot of people don't. No matter where we are in life, someone always has a bigger house than we do – or more money, or more talent, or happens to be better-looking. It may be painful to acknowledge, but someone always has more of *something* than we do.

But we can still love our lives as they are.

Should we strive for more? Should we work towards being the best possible version of ourselves? Absolutely. But along the way, we don't have to feel bitter, jealous, disappointed or disgruntled. There's no reason for that negativity.

I will grant you that maybe a little discontent is necessary – because that kernel of discontent does motivate you to make progress in your life. Feeling completely blissed out does blind you to making necessary improvements in your life and can make you complacent. But, again, at the same time, you can still love your life – and, just as importantly, love your potential for transforming the good things in your life into great things.

Here's what it comes down to – happiness is a state of mind.

I live in West Virginia where we've had a couple of brutal winters in recent years. Very cold and a LOT of snow. It can be fun for a while, but when February comes around, people get tired of bundling up and shoveling away the latest six inches of white stuff that just fell from the sky. They start complaining and each new cold snap worsens their moods.

And that's kind of silly when you think about it.

First of all, February means it's actually close to the end of winter – and that temperatures will soon be going up. More importantly, there is no way you can change the weather. Getting in a foul mood and complaining won't have one bit of impact on whether another blizzard will come your way or not – but it will have an impact on something more crucial.

And that's you.

When you get into a negative thinking pattern, your energy level goes down. Your tolerance for difficulties dissipates. Not only that, you're contagious. When you keep complaining about the weather to those around you, your bad mood infects other people. Soon, you've got an epidemic of irritability in your neighborhood and you're the Typhoid Mary that made it happen.

And, of course, you're definitely not loving your life.

That's when you should remember it's all in how you look at things. One of my favorite quotes is from George Santayana, a Spanish-American writer and philosopher who said a number of profound things. In this case, I love that he said, "To be interested in the changing seasons is a happier state of mind than to be hopelessly in love with the spring."

He's talking about the exact same thing I'm talking about in this chapter – that you should enjoy the process and variety of life, and avoid fixating on why things aren't perfect at the moment. It's having the ability to say to yourself, "You know what? It's the bitterly cold, snowy, blustery days in February that make me appreciate a beautiful spring day. If I only had beautiful spring days every day, I might get bored and take them for granted."

I don't mean to get bogged down in a weather debate (for instance, if you live in a tropical climate, you probably don't mind being in nonstop paradise, but to be truthful, I enjoy the variety). I just want to illustrate a point – which is that you can easily change your state of mind if you want to get beyond your own negativity, especially if that negativity is aimed at something you can't do anything about. And I'm going to share an exercise I learned long ago that can help you with your efforts. It's a simple exercise you can perform any time you feel the need.

For instance, let's pretend you're stuck in bad traffic. There are no alternate routes available and you're anxious about getting to the airport in time to make a flight. Just like the weather, there's nothing you can do about this disagreeable situation – you're stuck.

The worst part of it is the flight you're trying to catch is going to take you to someplace fun – for a weekend reunion with some old college pals that you've been looking forward to for a long time. And you don't want to miss a minute of it.

And yet, as you sit there staring at the same bumper in front of you that you've been staring at for an hour or so, you realize with a sinking feeling that you may actually miss that flight. The traffic jam seems to be getting worse, not better.

You grow more and more angry and frustrated. "Why is this happening to me?" you want to scream. Then, all of a sudden, you blink and, in a split-second, you're no longer in traffic.

You're in traction.

You're in a hospital bed and you can't move. You have no idea what's going on. Just a moment ago, you were driving your car to the airport. How the heck did this happen? You move your eyes downward – your entire body is in a cast. Just how badly hurt are you?

You move your eyes back up and see, entering your room, a few of your family members. They look devastated – tears are running down their faces. They fill in the blanks for you; it turns out you blacked out in the car and had a horrible accident. You can't remember anything about it and your mind is racing trying to put back the pieces of what happened.

"No, no," you weakly mutter, "This can't be happening. I was just driving to the airport. I was caught in traffic. How could something this awful happen?"

The family members explain. You had an accident and your car rolled down an embankment. Your injuries are very serious. And then comes the worst part.

The doctors aren't sure you'll ever walk again.

"I'm not going to be able to walk again?"

You feel woozy. You can feel that you've been heavily medicated, but waves of panic still overwhelm you. A nurse tells the family members they have to leave, because you need a lot of rest.

That's when something really weird happens.

Imagine, in this situation, after the room has emptied out, that someone else enters the room. Someone magical. It could be an angel, it could be a leprechaun, it could be Donald Trump, whatever works for you and your beliefs. Anyway, this magical being leans in close to you and whispers in your ear…

"I have the power to make this all go away."

That gets your attention. You're not sure if it's the painkillers talking, but you listen and you listen hard.

"I can make it as though the accident never happened – and these injuries will completely disappear."

"You can do all that?" you ask quietly in disbelief.

"Yes, I can. But there are two conditions."

"Two conditions? What are they?"

"Okay, here goes. Condition number one – you're going to be back in that horrible traffic jam, you're going to miss that flight and you're not going to be able to get on another one for a couple of days. Which means you'll completely miss seeing your old friends."

"And the other one?"

"Condition number two – you can't tell anyone about this conversation. Or about me. You can never tell anyone that the accident happened and then I fixed things so it didn't. This has to be our secret for the rest of your life."

"Okay."

"Okay? So we have a deal? You accept my terms?"

"Sure – what do I have to lose?"

Suddenly, you're back in that horrible traffic. Sure enough, you miss that flight and can't get on another one – everything is completely booked up. The first time around, that possibility enraged you, it made you feel like the entire world was against you and out to destroy your happiness.

Now – what's your mindset?

You probably feel ecstatic. Grateful. Like you literally just dodged a crippling bullet. You can *walk* – and you won't have to spend months and months regaining your strength and recovering from your injuries.

Exact same situation. Exact opposite mindset.

Here's another quote from another pretty good writer, a guy named Bill Shakespeare. In his play, *Hamlet*, the title character says, "…there is nothing either good or bad, but thinking makes it so."

That's what I'm talking about.

You have the power to change your mental attitude anytime you want. When you encounter a sudden shock of bad luck or any situation that's a great deal less than ideal, just think about something much worse happening to you. And then think about having the power to get back to where you are now and having that horrible thing completely go away.

That's how you practice a wonderful form of alchemy – transforming disappointment into gratitude, anger into joy and bitterness into an embrace of all the good things you currently enjoy.

So love your life as it is, warts and all.
And it will love you back.

SUPER SCORECARD #21

Superpower:	**Happiness**
Allows you to:	**Enjoy Your Life for Better or Worse**
Obtained by:	**Adjusting Your Attitude**
Arch Enemy:	**Negative Thinking**

MAKE MEMORABLE MOMENTS

Back in 1986, I went to see a movie entitled, *Ferris Bueller's Day Off,* a film that many in my generation (as well as a few others since then) enjoyed greatly.

Three decades later (let's not dwell on that!), one line in that film still resonates for a lot of people, including me. Matthew Broderick, playing the title role, says, "Life moves pretty fast. If you don't stop and look around once in a while, you might miss it."

Isn't that true.

That line is really in my head today, because it happens to be September 11th as I write these words. That date, of course, is the anniversary of America's most horrific tragedies that struck in New York City, Washington D.C. and in rural Pennsylvania. I can't even imagine what it's like on this day for the families of the 3000 people who lost their lives back in 2001. None of those victims, I'm sure, woke up that morning believing it would be the last day of their lives.

Life moves pretty fast. So stop every once in a while so you don't miss it.

Take a step back to reflect on your life. Think about your childhood and all those that loved and supported you. And maybe even double check those memories – I recently discovered that some of the things I remember may not have happened the way I thought they did, after talking to some other people who were also there at the time. That can be quite a shock – but there's no harm in hanging on to your version of events. They're your memories – so keep them and cherish them.

Besides – maybe *you're* right.

Now, take an extra step and examine those memories in detail. Recall the things you learned over the years, the takeaways you gained from hard-earned experience and continue to put those lessons to work today. Count your blessings – literally – and show gratitude for those blessings. You didn't come into this world with all you have today, and, even though you most likely worked hard to get everything you have, be grateful for those who helped you along the way.

And, finally, look at the memories you treasure the most. What made them so memorable? Why do you smile when you think about them?

Most importantly – how can you make more of them in the future? Not just for you – but for others around you?

Your family, friends and other loved ones. What makes your time with them the most enjoyable? Is it playing a game? Engaging in a physical sport? Or just talking around the fireplace? Focus on what makes those occasions the most special and try to replicate those conditions.

Then there are those that maybe need a little help – and I'm not talking about volunteering 8 hours a week (that's great to do if you have the time, of course), I'm talking about making small contributions. Save someone a parking spot. Let a car merge in front of you on the freeway. Help an elderly person across the street. Give directions to somebody who looks lost. If someone in front of you in a line at the cash register is a few coins short for a purchase, give it to them if you've got it.

You can create a good feeling in their lives – as well as yours – with the smallest acts of kindness. That's because little things add up.

We've spent a lot of time in this book discussing setting big goals and achieving mighty feats. That's what superheroes do, right? Well, not always. In the very first Superman movie starring Christopher Reeve, we follow the caped crusader on his first nightly patrol. He saves Lois Lane when she falls off the top off a high-rise, he foils a few big robberies, and saves a jumbo jet full of passengers when it's hit by lightning and the engines die.

But, in the very last scene of that sequence? It's not another huge action set piece that cost millions of dollars. No, it's simple a little girl who is crying because her cat is stuck high up in a tree. Superman flies to the rescue, carefully grabs the cat and returns it safely.

The movie's message? Doing that small favor for that girl was just as important as all those other giant heroic acts.

Big is important. Big is cool. But big takes a while. It takes effort. It takes a lot of thought and a lot of work.

In contrast, little is easy. You can do a little every day – and it will end up adding up to a lot, both to you and those around you. It's a perfect way to create memorable moments on a regular basis, and it usually takes a minimum of time and effort.

So let me end this chapter by issuing one more challenge.

Within the next hour, do something nice for someone. Don't do it because you're going to get anything back, just do it for the sake of doing it. And, again, this doesn't have to be a grandiose act of benevolence. Recently, I held the hand of an elderly woman who needed help walking out of a basketball game – that kind of thing counts. So does paying for someone's coffee. Or putting some coins in someone's parking meter that you notice is about to expire. Or buying some cookies from a Girl Scout.

Imagine if everybody in the world took this challenge every day. Imagine billions of kind acts happening every 24 hours – kind acts that wouldn't have happened otherwise. Imagine how that would improve the energy on this planet.

Now *that* would be a memorable moment.

SUPER SCORECARD #22

Superpower:	**Helping Those Around You**
Allows you to:	**Make the World a Better Place**
Obtained by:	**Random Acts of Kindness**
Arch Enemy:	**Disregard**

AFTERWORD: FINISH STRONG!

I don't usually repeat advice from fortune cookies – but, as I finish up this book, there's one solid piece of wisdom that pops up on a regular basis inside those wrapped-in-plastic treats.

The fortune I'm talking about goes like this: *Life always gets harder near the summit.*

It's true. When you read about those brutal ascents to the top of Mount Everest, the climbers nearly always say that they're too tired to really enjoy the view from the peak. Plus, the air's so thin, they have to hurry down before they pass out!

Of course, the fortune isn't just about mountain climbing (technically, it isn't even a fortune, but don't get me started on that). It's a metaphor that, simply stated, means any genuinely great effort becomes the most difficult just as you're about to complete it.

Let's talk one more time about our superhero pals. I think you'll agree that, when you see one of their movies, you know that the biggest battle will come near the end of the film. That's when it looks like they'll never survive the fight against the evil all-powerful bad guy. But they reach deep down into themselves – and they prevail.

Yes, I realize that represents a bunch of screenwriters pulling the strings, but it resonates because there's some truth to the idea. You have a huge goal – you work hard to achieve it – and naturally, some exhaustion and impatience sets in as you close in on reaching your objective. A thousand details overwhelm you at once, because, as you do near completion, you want to make sure nothing goes wrong. So you can't neglect any one of the details, because if you do, it could be end up being the weak link in the chain of all the hard work you've done – a weak link that snaps in two and ends up dooming all your efforts.

That's why you always need to *finish strong.*

The people that are the most successful, the happiest, the biggest winners in life? They run through the finish line, they don't walk. They don't become complacent and assume a guaranteed victory. Instead, they guarantee that victory for themselves by saving their maximum effort for the final lap.

So, as I close out this book, I challenge you to finish strong in all your endeavors. And that includes the end of the year, traditionally the time for celebrating, relaxing and reflecting on the 12 months that have just gone by. Now, all of that is important…but the end of the year is also a great time to ensure that you finish strong – and prepare the way for a great new year.

Here are three ways you can do just that:

1. Keep playing hard.

Heading into the holidays, it's easy to take your foot off the gas pedal and cruise through the last few weeks of the year. But that year is not yet over – and neither is the business you should be doing. There are still relationships to attend to and future work to line up. Don't let the holiday rush of parties and shopping get in the way of all business activity. When it's time to shut it down for the holidays, by all means, turn off your smartphone and enjoy this special time of the year. But until that moment comes, keep giving it your all. Remember the football players who hold up four fingers at the beginning of the final quarter, who indicate with that gesture that, "You know what? It's not over until it's over. It's no time to be tired. Let's all keep going through the final whistle that signals the end of the game."

2. Keep planning ahead.

When the end of December rolls around, the people who are looking back on the most successful years are the people who, twelve months earlier, took the time to make a great plan. Most people don't go into a new year with a detailed outline of what kind of outcomes they want to realize and what strategies they're going to employ to create those outcomes. I'm not just talking about financial results, by the way, I'm also talking about your health, your relationships, your family life, and your intellectual and spiritual development. In whatever areas you feel are lacking, create specific goals and realistic plans for what you're going to do on a daily basis to make the upcoming year one of your best.

3. Engage in enjoyment.

I'm sure as you read that subheading, you said to yourself, "Ed wants me to engage in enjoyment? Why wouldn't I?" Well, you'd be surprised who wouldn't – or maybe not, once I explain what I'm talking about. Many people, once they start their holiday vacations, simply shut down all together. Men especially begin staring like zombies at every single football bowl game that shows up on television, even though they really don't have a vested interest in whether Bowling Green beats South Alabama in the Raycom Media Camellia Bowl or if Illinois beats Louisiana Tech in the Zaxby's Heart of Dallas Bowl. No offense to any fans of those schools, but most Americans don't really have dogs in those hunts.

What I advocate is actively participating in activities with your family and friends – or even volunteering and giving to other people. Engage with those around you – it's not only a gift to them, you'll find it's a gift to you as well.

In conclusion, I'd like to quote another related fortune cookie: *The man on the top of the mountain did not fall there.*

In other words, that guy had to *climb* to the top - and if you want to reach the top of the mountain, you've got to do some climbing of your own.

But that climb is totally worth the effort.

I hope every single one of you reading this book will take its advice to heart – and will put it to work in order to release *your* superhero. I do believe there's an incredible amazing and mighty super-powered person inside of all of us – but too many of us leave that hero sitting in there, twiddling his or her thumbs, waiting endlessly for the chance to leap into action.

Don't let your superhero wait any longer.

You may not have your own billion-dollar movie franchise and you may not even have your own skintight multicolored costume (if you do, I would suggest you only wear it indoors…), but, if you apply the principles I've explained in this book, you can indeed reach your own super-level of achievement.

You *can* fulfill your goals faster than a speeding bullet. You *can* create a business more powerful than a locomotive. And you *can* leap over your competition in a single bound. All it takes is the right plan, an unshakeable commitment to your goals, and the follow-through that will take you all the way to your ultimate success.

So here's to truth, justice and the American way.

Here's to you, hero.

ABOUT ED DECOSTA

Ed DeCosta, who previously authored *Ascend: A Coach's Roadmap for Taking Your Performance to New Heights*, is President of Catalyst Associates LLC, an executive coaching and management consulting firm. Catalyst Associates helps clients set and achieve smart goals, enabling them to meet their personal and business objectives. Clients range from small entrepreneurial ventures to Fortune 500 corporations.

In his corporate life, Ed managed worldwide sales and marketing teams and opened offices on three continents. He is presently working as a partner with best-selling author and leadership guru John C. Maxwell, serving as one of the faculty members in the Maxwell Leadership Development Program.

He is an ICF certified professional coach, has a B.S. in Mechanical Engineering from West Virginia University and a Master's Degree in International Management and MBA from the University of Texas. Ed is also an adjunct faculty member in WVU's College of Business and Economics, teaching Professional Selling and Entrepreneurship courses.

Ed DeCosta does not claim to be Superman, but he does believes the Man of Steel could benefit from his coaching skills. Ed and his own personal Wonder Woman, wife Linda, live in Morgantown, WV.

44321679R00108

Made in the USA
Charleston, SC
22 July 2015